D0421916

SHE CAN
Laugh
AT THE DAYS
TO COME

Books by Valerie Bell

Reaching Out to Lonely Kids
*Coming Back: Real-Life Stories of Courage from
    Spiritual Survivors*
Getting Out of Your Kids' Faces and into Their Hearts

valerie bell

SHE CAN
Laugh
AT THE DAYS
TO COME

STRENGTHENING THE SOUL
FOR THE JOURNEY AHEAD

❧

ZondervanPublishingHouse
Grand Rapids, Michigan

A Division of HarperCollins*Publishers*

She Can Laugh at the Days to Come
Copyright © 1996 by Valerie Bell

Requests for information should be addressed to:

ZondervanPublishingHouse
Grand Rapids, Michigan 49530

Library of Congress Cataloging-in-Publication Data

Bell, Valerie, 1949–   .
      She can laugh at the days to come: strengthening the soul for the journey
ahead / Valerie Bell.
            p.   cm.
      Includes bibliographical references (p.   ).
      ISBN: 0-310-20569-7
      1. Women—Religious life.   2. Women—Conduct of life.   I. Title.
BV4527.B4   1996
248.8'43—dc20   96-24795
                                                                                      CIP

This edition printed on acid-free paper and meets the American National
Standards Institute Z39.48 standard.

Interior design by Sherri L. Hoffman

Printed in the United States of America

---

97 98 99 00 01 02 03 /❖ DH/ 10 9 8 7 6 5 4 3

To Steve
The husband of my youth.
The husband of my middle years.
Grow old along with me.
The best is yet to be.

Contents

Acknowledgments

Applause!

A book is a team project. My name may appear in the author spot on the spine, but these pages reflect the effort of many others as well. I am truly grateful for the thought and care given to this project. My sincere applause and thanks!

Thanks to Bruce Zabel for his wise guidance through the business maze of publishing. He has been a tremendous help to me.

Thanks to Sandy Vander Zicht for her sound advice on this book's focus, and for believing that my ideas merit publishing.

Thanks to Rachel Boers for her professionalism and for sticking with the editing details.

And finally, special thanks to Evelyn Bence, a creative writer in her own right, but also my editor on this book. Evelyn, your input motivated me to work harder, bleed some, and laugh more. You were invaluable to me. Thank you! Thank you!

Let the Laughter Begin

❧

This is a book about developing soul, the spiritual issues of becoming.

Soul brother, soul food, soul kiss, soul music, soul-searching, soul mate; our culture uses *soul* as an adjective to describe things that are deep, sensitive, and profound. But *soul* is also a noun. A soul is the immaterial essence of one's being, one's intrinsic and eternal self. For the most part, our souls are neglected.

But no one ages successfully while ignoring the soul. Early in life we must become aware of how we are forming spiritually. It is never too early to begin to invest in the process of caring for our souls. It is never too early to begin acknowledging that we are, indeed, aging.

"How can you write a book about aging when you're not that old yet?" a male friend asked.

I smiled at what was meant as a compliment. It was a good question, and I gave a simple answer that summarizes the book I was writing—this book. It is not about *being* old but about *becoming* old. Whether we are twenty or ninety years old, we are aging. In the film *What About Bob?* the psychologist's morose young son had it right; with eyes opened wide in alarm, he said,

"We are all dying." He did not mean that we are all dead; he simply was stating the awesome emerging awareness of the knowledge that we are all in the process. Exactly. We are not all old, but we are all in the process.

Most of us are keenly aware of the issues of the aging body. But how many of us are as keenly aware of the issues of the aging soul? Wrinkles and menopause and osteoporosis are the backdrops, not the main focus, in this perspective on aging.

She Can Laugh at the Days to Come is unabashedly feminine. The brave men who read it will probably benefit from the focus once they get over the feeling of having wandered into the women's locker room. Women, this book is primarily for you. We need special help in our "process of becoming," because the world does not make it easy for us to let go of our youth. Our feminine souls must be strong enough to thrive in a culture where our stock plummets with our first wrinkle, our first age spot, our first gray hair.

As I was finishing this book, I read a magazine article in which a woman complained that she had not yet read a good book on aging. My feelings exactly! My hope is that *She Can Laugh at the Days to Come* will make a contribution to a void in our thinking about the second half of our life journeys. My intention is that you will laugh as you travel with me for a while. I hope you will also, along with that delight, feel a strong pull toward deeper, more connected, soulful living. You may see your soul clearly for the very first time in these pages. You may recognize yourself and your female friends in the Red-Hot Mama. You will meet soul's slaver and soul's cannibal.

The title *She Can Laugh at the Days to Come* is from Proverbs 31. In these pages I trust you will grow to appreciate the incredible significance of that descriptive phrase. To me it is the most amazing thing ever said about a woman. Above all else, may you find yourself fitting your soul for all eternity through attention to the issues of your feminine soul in the here and now.

To the women! Here's to you! In the days to come may you have the incredible soul strength to throw your head back, lift your eyes to heaven, and laugh.

One

❧

How Did Mother Get into My Mirror?

I remember my youth and that feeling that will never come back anymore—the feeling that I could outlast forever, outlast the sea, the earth, and all men; the deceitful feeling that lures us on to joys, to perils, to love, to vain effort—to death; the triumphant conviction of strength, the heat of life in the handful of dust, the glow in the heart that with every year grows dim, grows cold, grows small, and expires—and expires, too soon, too soon—before life itself.

—Joseph Conrad, *Youth*

$\mathcal{I}$t was my fortieth birthday. In Wheaton, Illinois, my hometown, it was a normal day, just another day to conduct business as usual and get on with suburban life. A fortieth birthday isn't, after all, exactly front-page headline news. It won't even get your picture on the *Today Show* with Willard Scott ... you have to do more than twice the living for that perk. It's no big deal. Ho-hum. Everyone knows it's nothing.

Everyone, that is, except people who are turning forty. Deep in their hearts they know that although the world has marched on without a pause, their life has just turned a corner and certain things will never be the same.

My heart knew. After all, a fortieth birthday can hardly be just another plain-Jane, nothing-has-changed, regular day for most women passing that birthday milestone. It was now official. I was undeniably, unretractably, unbelievably middle-aged.

I consoled myself with the bleak comfort that at least my thirty-ninth year was over and done with. What a rotten year that had been! Nine months before my fortieth birthday I had left my doctor's office with his cancer diagnosis of malignant melanoma, a potentially fatal skin cancer, ringing in one ear and his odd final words ringing in the other, "Valerie, the most important advice I can give you about your health today is to be sure you wear your seat belt." What did he mean? Buckle up, I heard. Today is all any of us is guaranteed. All bets are off on tomorrow. Concentrate on today and get ready for the ride of your life!

That year, that last year of my "youth," was unlike any I had ever experienced. An operation cut out the cancer, my prognosis was excellent, but to my great distress, I found no cure for the fear that had entered my life with the "C" word. Despite assurances that I would survive this disease, I slipped into a world where the Androcles' sword of cancer and potential death hung over me. My waking thoughts were of cancer. It robbed me of my sleep and my usual sense of well-being. I was fragile and sad. My focus became concentrated and immediate. I stopped making plans for the future and dreaming dreams that might be too painful not to see realized. Reading, a lifelong passion, proved too demanding. I could not concentrate on ideas. I learned to cross-stitch. Boy, did I cross-stitch! 1, 2 . . . 1, 2 . . . Up, down . . . filled my conscious mind. Absorption therapy. Ah! the year of my cross-stitching. The year of my lost mind!

This fortieth birthday might not have been. Looking back now, across cancer-free years, I have perspective on that difficult time. Cancer was attacking my body, but fear was ravaging my soul. My body was out of trouble long before my soul. Recently my college-aged philosophy major son, Brendan, casually passed on this piece of knowledge. "You know, Mom," he informed me, "there are two types of fear. One fear is a reaction to a real stress." (Cancer in my case, or to any actual experience—being mugged, experiencing a car accident, or living through an earthquake.) He continued, waxing philosophical, "The second kind of fear is anxiety. If fear is the reaction to what *has* happened, anxiety is a fear of what *might* happen." He summarized it succinctly, "Anxiety is a fear of living."

"Oh learn-ed one! I think you are onto something there!" I smiled at my child turned wise.

I should know. His definition precisely captured my dilemma when I turned forty. More than life being simply pre-forty and postforty, my life had a definite divide of precancer, postcancer. The defining difference was fear. I was afraid of dying, but oddly, I was almost more afraid of living. If I continued to live, how could I face the "days to come" with the kind of interior strength needed to deal with all that life could throw at me? If life could be this fragile and frightening at thirty-nine and forty, how terrible was seventy going to be? Just like the body becomes hypervigilant with an adrenaline flood in response to fearful stimuli, my soul had gone on hyperalert. It was safety-belted and slamming on the brakes to stop living fully. Dangerous curves ahead! Beware of falling rocks! Reduce speed! Bumps! Potholes! Steep cliffs and slippery pavements ahead!

I was forty and I was afraid of life!

My concerned friends used my birthday as an excuse to try to cheer me out of my depression. That morning a friend had given me a birthday brunch. Sitting in her dining room sharing the day with our mutual friends, I was aware of receiving more than my normal share of birthday care. Later that day at home I noticed a larger than usual pile of birthday cards waiting for me on the dining room table.

It was the "kid-glove" treatment. My family was getting particularly good at handling my fragility. It had been a long nine months for them as well. Justin, our younger son, was a sponge for my sadness. He could feel my pain. Several times a day he would ask me, "Mom, are you sad?" He wanted his happy mother back. It broke my heart to hurt him in such a way. On this, my fortieth birthday, we would try to put death in the wings and celebrate life. My husband, Steve, the Associate Director of a nationally syndicated Christian broadcast, left work earlier than normal that day and he and our two sons prepared a birthday meal. During shrimp scampi (amazing!) and before birthday cake, I opened the pile of cards. I easily recognized the charming grade-school scrawl of our ten-year-old son, Justin, and the artistic penmanship of his fourteen-year-old brother, Brendan. All the cards were incredibly funny. How come everyone's so funny when you might be dying?

I groaned when I opened the card from my older sister. "Congratulations!" the front said—a message bland enough for any birthday. I wasn't sufficiently prepared for the jab inside …"another year closer to looking like Mom!"

Only a sister would think such a card appropriate to give a potentially dying woman. Only an older sister who is happy to see the signs of aging in a younger sister. Well, after all, better to see the signs of aging than the signs of dying. And then I grinned. It is not easy to get a depressed woman to laugh, but this card did. I laughed right out loud despite a twinge of guilt that reminded me that our deceased mother would not have enjoyed this joke at her expense.

Anticipating a few laughs, I set it aside to show it to several forty-something friends. After all, is there a middle-aged woman who cannot appreciate the twisted humor in the nearly universal feminine fear—*I'm starting to look like my mother?*

Here was a new thought. I might live. But I might live to look like Mom. My mother was thirty-seven when I was born. As far as I could remember, she was always older than my friends' moms. She had "problem" hair—gray dyed to various shades of brassy brown; it just never was quite right. She was round, not lean. Her beautiful eyes were diminished by deep circles. Her later years were wrinkled and jowled.

Cancer had forced me to care for my body, focusing on preventative measures against its return. I was more body aware than I had ever been before. But even as I laughed about my sister's prediction, I was reminded of another kind of body care. What were people seeing when they looked at me? As I held that card, it was a remindful grid through which I remembered incidents passed. Another year closer to looking like Mom? It was a comment I was hearing more and more often. Mother's relatives and friends were saying, "Oh, you look so much like Wilma!" They meant it as an affectionate compliment. Now with my sister's prediction in hand, I heard it differently.

What was my sister seeing? What was it about me that reminded my mother's friends of her?

Some incidents came to mind. I remembered my surprise when I caught a glimpse of my backside in the three-way mirror of a changing room. *Whoa! What was this?* I had a rare view of myself from every angle. It was Mother in my mirror. Well, well, well! Talk about a resurrection! Even a casual examination revealed that I was both sagging and dimpled. *When did my derriere start looking like last year's orange?* I did not remember looking like that *last* swimsuit season. *Thank heaven for clothes!* Modesty has a lot of incentives for a middle-aged woman. I would be covering more of this body in the days to come.

I remembered some recent unflattering snapshots of me. I had brushed them aside as the result of weird camera angles or unflattering light. Now I had to consider a new possibility. Perhaps the camera had been faithful. I dug the pictures out from the bottom of the reject pile. I scrutinized the puffy face and the dark-circled eyes. *It was Wilma! When had this happened?*

It was the changing-room experience all over again. The camera had definitely recorded a tendency toward a softening chin line, the beginning of jowls. I looked faded and out of focus. I was rounder than I remembered. Could it be that my hair was really that dull, my expression that taunt and tired?

Just the previous weekend something had happened that gave me a little jolt. The college-aged pizza delivery boy had called me "ma'am." It jarred me. I know what "ma'am" means. Young men do not call cute young chickies "ma'am." It is a euphemism they politely hide behind when they think you are not really a living breathing woman but a fossilized specimen from the antediluvian period. What they are really thinking is *How did she survive the flood?* They say "ma'am"; they mean "old relic." *Oh heartless boy*, I winced, *what you communicated in one "respectful" word should be against the law.*

It was just one more indicator that as an aging woman, my stock was going down. At forty, I was beginning to experience the downward mobility of an aging body, an aging body prone to disease.

In my forties I could no longer live in denial. My body was failing me on several levels. Oh body, what a traitor you are! Even a "you-look-young-for-your-age" face cannot console a woman for the loss felt when the mirror reflects not only horizontal lines but also vertical crosshatch lines, a living, breathing checkerboard in the flesh. Even a "you-look-young-for-your-age" face cannot console a woman for the loss of health and beauty and perceived worth.

Catching a glimpse of my future, seeing my mother in my mirror penetrated what was left of my defenses. Is this all I have to look forward to as I age, if I age? Everybody sing!

> *Happy Birthday to me!*
> *Happy Birthday to me!*
> *I'm aging like Mother.*
> *Depression! Misery!*

Ecclesiastes 12 describes in vivid poetic language the degeneration that accompanies old age. The Jewish exegetist, Maurice Jastrow, gives an insightful commentary on the biblical passage. It's a long, hard look into the mirror of our futures.

> Remember now thy Creator in the days of thy youth, while the evil days come not, nor the years draw nigh, when thou shalt say, I have no pleasure in them; while the sun, or the light, or the moon, or the stars, be not darkened, nor the clouds return after the rain [diminution of the sight, extinction of intellectual powers] in the day when the keepers of the house [the arms] shall tremble, and the strong men [the legs] shall bow themselves, and the grinders [the teeth] cease because they are few, and those that look out of the windows [the eyes] be darkened, and the doors shall be shut in the streets [digestive and

urinary difficulties], when the sound of grinding is low [deafness], and he shall rise up at the voice of the bird [poor sleep, early wakening], and all the daughters of musick shall be brought low [difficulties in speech]; also when they shall be afraid of that which is high [breath-lessness in going up stairs or slopes], and fears shall be in the way, and the almond tree shall flourish [white hair], and the grasshopper shall be a burden [fading of sexual power].... Or ever the silver cord be loosed [bending of the spinal column], or the golden bowl be broken, or the pitcher be broken at the fountain, or the wheel be broken at the cistern [malfunction of the liver and kidneys] ... [1]

Mercy! And to think my biggest worry about aging was that I was starting to look like Mom!

A new thought emerges. *Maybe I will not only look like her; maybe I will eventually be older than she.* Mom was only sixty-nine when she died. Someday I may hear the words, "You look so much like your mother," as a compliment.

Denial About the Days to Come

Someone has said, "Aging, like dying, is something a person can get good at not thinking about."[2] It is so true. Actually, our culture, in an amazing example of groupthink, excels at not thinking about growing older. Or we consciously calculate ways to fight it. The real American national sport is not baseball, not football, not even basketball, but age wrestling! Americans invest incredible life energy in keeping our bodies well-oiled, primed, and behaving as young as possible. Beneath the societal chutzpah and hoopla, however, lurks a dark reality. While we are characterized as a culture that worships youth, the dark side of that coin is our fear of age and death. Many fortunes have been made by exploiting this primal fear. Promises such as "Instant Age Eraser" and "Reverse the Aging Process" beckon (successfully it appears) from the covers of women's magazines. This denial of ultimate reality is encouraged to the maximum by those who stand to profit.

Why do we buy into this approach? Being "suckered" is the price many are willing to pay for denial. So while we would rather not be reminded, the eventual benefits of all this working out, the swallowing of antioxidants, slathering of alpha hydroxyl creams, low-fat dieting, sweating, pumping, and sliding, and the spending of big bucks can be summed up succinctly: We might look younger than the next person, but we will eventually experience that blessing while wearing a coffin.

Care of self is an appropriate goal. But too often in our culture, care of self is interpreted exclusively as care of the body. Entrepreneurs and corporations are eager to make money off those who simply don't want to think about the realities of living, aging, and dying.

In contrast, the message we sometimes receive from more spiritual sources is that growing older really should not bother us at all. This is the if-you-were-more-spiritual-it-wouldn't-bother-you approach to aging. It's hard to imagine saints like Mother Teresa, Amy Carmichael, or Margaret Fells (a Quaker prison reformer)—or any number of unheralded women whose pioneer work opened mission fields, established orphanages, and cared for the poor—mourning smooth skin turned permanently pleated and splotchy with age spots.

We tell ourselves that truly spiritual women aren't concerned with the body's decline. And we hear it from other spiritual experts: "Live above it! It's only body!" It's as if the body and whatever happens to it is unimportant. This attitude is also denial. It fits a hair shirt over our wounds. Being expected to wrap ourselves in spiritual piety while ignoring the real issues of aging makes the challenging journey of the second half of life more painful and confusing than it needs to be.

A Distinctive Christian View of Aging

What attitude should we then adopt about growing older? We need an approach that will be honest enough to admit that growing older can be an overwhelming process. We deserve that dignity. We also need the comfort from the recognition that our sense of loss, our struggle with the process, is appropriate, not simply vanity. We need hope that we will be able to surmount any changes the future holds. We need models of courage, not models of denial for the challenging days to come. My feeling is this: It is better to take the long, hard look into the mirror of the future and not be caught off guard. We take a healthy step when we can admit to being a participant in the process.

Whether our birthday cakes glow sweetly with sixteen candles or blaze with a bonfire of seventy-eight, we are experiencing the growing-older process. If we can stop dealing with "Am I aging?" we can begin to deal with the greater issue, "*How* am I aging?"

Facing the days to come, we can have hope if we understand that we are so much more than body. We are body and soul. We were created to operate with two realities: inner—spiritual, and outer—physical, including our appearance and health. It is a gift to know that truth. Even though it is sad that our bodies are temporary, the upside is the understanding that we are so much more than body.

A group of us were talking about this after aerobics class one day. All of us were "of a certain" age, sweaty and exhausted from an hour of energetic work. One woman reminded me, "I care for my body for more than body. I care for my body because there are quality of life issues. I don't want only to live longer, I want to stay as healthy as possible for as long as possible."

She is right. Quality of life was why I was exercising too. But there are limits to the benefits derived from caring for our bodies. In the years after cancer, I learned to take much better care of my body. But caring for my body did not release me from the anxiety that gripped my life and robbed me of joy. Caring for my body did not restore a confidence about life. It did not replace my tears with laughter nor did it open me to a deeper level of living. Learning to care for my soul was what healed my wounded self. No body work, be it cosmetic or health-oriented, can heal the soul in an aging woman's life.

Tend the body, but be realistic enough to admit that your body will never be as good at seventy as it was at seventeen. Grieve if you must, but be aware of an emerging wonderful reality—you are more than body, and new possibilities and potentials are opening to you. Care for your soul and you can be better at seventy than you were at seventeen. Care for your soul and you have made an enormous stride toward quality living. Care of the soul is the approach to aging that will help us manage the days to come with confidence, joy, and inner strength.

The good news is that the days to come need not be a wasteland. The process of aging offers an opportunity, a new invitation to shift our focus to include care for our eternal selves. In the past few years I have noticed that my attitude about aging has shifted. I am seeing it much more as a spiritual "becoming" than just as a process of loss. This perspective has filled me with a hopeful anticipation that the future holds many "soulful" opportunities.

Predictions for an Ignored Soul

And yet it seems that a well-cared-for soul is more rare than we would like to believe. That is too bad. The various forms of denial encourage women to ignore the issues of the aging feminine soul. Ignored souls bring predictable results. If Ecclesiastes 12 had been written about the aging of the untended soul, it might have warned of the typical signs: the loneliness and regrets, the bitterness and depression, the self-centeredness and envy and anger. The untended soul complicates and corrupts our look at the future. The neglected soul is uglier than anything our mirrors could in time reflect back to us. The true measure of how we are doing is not our reflection in the mirror, but rather, the reflection of our souls.

A woman who neglects her intrinsic self predictably ages like a manicured rock. No depth. No character. No redeeming qualities that can make the most life-weathered, female octogenarian attractive.

Or worse. Will the weathering and wearing of life embitter you, fill you with regrets, and sour you? Will your life produce vinegar from its fruits? Overlook the spiritual issues, neglect your soul, and you will age like a lipsticked toxic dump site!

Meet a Well-Aged Woman

As you look at the future, consider a spiritual dimension. Attention to the details of the developing soul define those who age well. Paul Theroux, the travel writer, wrote, "The greatest travel always contains within it the seeds of a spiritual quest."[3] He was speaking of another kind of journey, and yet the same principle applies to the journey of life. As we travel through the calendar, we must tend to our souls as we blow out the candles.

Our spiritual quest is to seek a deeper, more developed inner self. I challenge you to grow wiser, even as you let go of the potentiality of youth. Put meaning into the rings of your life tree. Mellow. Sweeten. Lighten. Strengthen. Deepen.

I look to an extraordinary woman for help as I approach the unfamiliar future. She comes right out of the pages of the Bible. She has no name. She is known simply as the Proverbs 31 woman. Some have tried to make her seem less intimidating by claiming that she was never a real person, just an ideal. That may be, but I have known—been both inspired and intimidated by—many women who come awfully close to imitating her.

The extended description of this woman includes many aspects. For example, "her husband has full confidence in her." In our house that would mean my husband would never have to ask, "How much was check number 1221?" Unlike Valerie Bell, the Proverbs 31 woman would always write the amount in the ledger. Amazing! (I prefer to keep my husband guessing.)

How about this? "She gets up while it is still dark and provides food for her family." If you aren't an "oh-what-a-beautiful-morning" type, don't worry. Think of this another way. Note that the writer of Proverbs fails to describe this woman at 10:00 P.M., when her internal lights are long extinguished, but you're just getting your second wind!

Whether you love this woman or find her a compulsive overachiever, I challenge you to examine more closely one of her lesser-praised characteristics. To me, it is the most amazing thing ever written about any person—man or woman: "She can laugh at the days to come."

It appears as a throwaway. *Oh, and by the way, if she has not impressed you yet, let me just mention in passing, "She can laugh at the days to come"!*

Ha! That's me, all right! Secure and full of a sense of well-being, especially when I think about the possibility of my cancer coming back. I just consider menopause, and I get kind of tickled thinking about those hot flashes with accompanying mood swings to come. What about osteoporosis? That just makes me want to throw my head back and laugh like a loon!

She can laugh at the days to come? Amazing!

Picture this woman. Her gray head is thrown back, lifting toward heaven a deeply wrinkled face. Her jowls shake like Jell-O. Her mouth widens in laughter, exposing teeth perfected by dentures. Her breasts sag, her belly bulges, her legs are marbled with blue rivulets cresting their banks, and her dimples have long ago disappeared, buried deeply in wrinkles, but somehow she seems incredibly attractive. She "youngs" before your very eyes, her spirit shining through. Even while experiencing deteriorating health and beauty, she laughs. Though frail, she lets laughter rip through her body. She laughs with confidence, with spunk, abandon, and class. It is a fine and incredible sound, the sound of laughter in the face of death.

She is beautiful. Don't you see? Even if you found her intimidating or struggled to identify with her in the past, you have to love and admire her when you picture her this way.

She is not afraid of what lies ahead. She embraces "the days to come." She is confident, formidable even in the face of the ultimate reality of death. She knows she is in the "ma'am" stage of life. She does not care. She would not trade her hard-won wisdom and life perspective for a wink from the pizza boy any day.

This is the spiritual quest I have set for myself. It is the plucky quality I want to achieve in the second half of my life journey.

I want to age well. I refuse to deny it or fight it. I want to master it. I too want to be an intimidating woman to take down.

I want to throw my head back and confidently laugh in the face of the unknown. I want to confuse the evil plans of the Enemy by my uncommon response. I want muscles on my soul that flex mightily even if the reflection in the mirror says I am not doing so well.

One year closer to looking like Mom? I want to blister age's ears with my laughing response to that one! One year closer to the reality of death? Yes. But I have a plan of my own.

I intend to have the last laugh!

Two

Soul Mirrors: Having Your True Colors Done by Trevor the Terrible

Some fear the passage of time.
Others welcome it because it will reveal their strengths.

—Car commercial

An angry middle-aged person is usually a jerk.

—Unknown

*Y*ou can look in a mirror to discover the truth about your physical aging, but where can you go to find out the truth about how your soul is developing? How can you tell if your soul is aging well? The truth about the soul's progression can be found in unpredictable, even perverse places. We can catch the truth about our inner reality in snatches of conversation, feedback that gives us clues about how we are doing spiritually. Soul mirrors are everywhere, but often where we least expect them.

Let me explain how I learned the realities of my soul's development. It was not a minister or a spiritual advisor of some kind who helped me see the truth. Strangely, it took a hairdresser to hold a mirror up to my middle-aged soul to show me the truth about myself. His name was Trevor. He is the owner of his own hair studio. For a period of time he did my hair. Surprisingly, he also did my soul.

Trevor was an "artiste." He prided himself on his sense of style and taste in high fashion. He was a fashion cognoscente, ironically condemned to live and work in our little penny-loafer suburb. I, in contrast, was a young "spiritual" woman. I prided myself on not caring too much about trivia such as fashion. The last thing I was interested in was looking like something that slithered down a fashion runway in Paris! Almost from the beginning we were headed for a collision.

It was extremely fashionable some years ago to have your colors "done." Men and women would go to a color consultant to be given an analysis of their skin tone, hair, and eye color. Then they were given (for what I thought was a hefty fee) color swatches that would complement their natural coloring. The theory was that by having your colors done, you could select and organize your wardrobe, putting your best colorized self forward at all times.

I thought it was baloney. To me, it smacked of a money-making scheme that took advantage of women's insecurities.

I was in my early thirties. Years before, my father had survived a bout with encephalitis but it had burned up his brain, leaving him in a vegetable-like state for four-and-a-half years. He died when I was thirty. And then, only two years later, my mother died from a massive heart attack. I think this was not only the saddest but also the most dowdy time of my life. Looking back, I realize my low-grade depression affected my outlook.

To my discredit, however, I managed to put a spiritual twist on my whole lackluster approach. I would not have my colors done. Instead, I would dress for my soul—wearing what I "felt" like wearing—not what someone armed with swatches and greed told me to wear. Proudly, I wore my navy blues and browns like a badge of spiritual superiority. I guess I could call it my "Protestant nun" stage. Spiritual is serious, you know, and I had serious spiritual work to do. My life would be uncluttered by trivial color pursuits. Without question, there was more than a little touch of spiritual snobbery in my attitude!

In this frame of mind, I began to go to Trevor to have my hair done. (No-nonsense-nun-short, of course. What else?) He had a reputation; everyone said he gave the best haircut in the suburbs. With my genetic tendency toward mostly "bad hair" days, I decided to get the most help I could find.

From his snakeskin boots to his highlighted-blond ponytail, Trevor oozed a kind of worldliness that always made me feel extremely out of place in his salon, excuse me, studio. Complicating matters was his approach to women. Trevor was macho, superior, aloof. Attempts on my part to strike up a conversation with him usually received one-word responses, if that. As he silently worked, he always pulled a little too hard on my hair. He never made eye contact or acted as if he had seen me before, even though I was one of his regular customers. He rarely spoke, except to inform me of how he thought I *should* be wearing my hair. Usually the only way he acknowledged my presence at all was by poking me in the back with his finger. And I wasn't the only one. He had a way of letting most of his clients know that he was unimpressed that they were there.

But his shop was booked solid.

What was this man's appeal? How did he keep his clientele? What was keeping me coming back? Why do women stay with men who treat us so poorly? In all my visits to his shop he had never asked me one question about myself. Apparently I was just another head of hair. I began to think of him as Trevor the

Terrible. But I didn't leave. I could stand an hour of discomfort in exchange for a great haircut, I rationalized. I dealt with this awkward situation by becoming increasingly quiet and distant with Trevor. I wanted in and out, fast!

Trevor was not going to let me off the hook so easily. Without subtlety, Trevor informed me about my great need for his services as a color consultant. He began to talk to me. "That color looks bad on you. You should never wear it." Or "That lipstick is too coral for your skin; you should definitely stick with rose tones." Ha! He should have been glad I was wearing lipstick at all—it isn't, after all, the usual style of Protestant nuns! It was as though I were being beaten up by a fashion bully every time I went to his shop.

Worst of all, he began to talk to me about his other customers. "See that woman over there?" he nodded across the room. "She looks terrible in that sweater."

I thought she looked fine. Baiting him, I asked, "Well, why don't you cue her in like you're always cueing me?"

He answered with bald frankness, his voice dripping with disdain, "Because I don't like her enough to tell her."

Oh, he was too much! I scolded myself for paying for and listening to this kind of abuse. And even while I considered the distinct possibility that this would be my last visit to Trevor's house of horrors, in the middle of that very thought, he landed his coup de grace to my soul.

Out of nowhere he suddenly blurted out: "Why are you so angry?"

I looked up to see whom he was addressing. He was looking straight at me. The question was accompanied by a pleased-with-himself grin. This was an experienced chain-puller of women. He knew exactly what he was doing.

"What?" I asked incredulously. "Are you talking to me?"

"Yes! Why are you so angry?" His smile reeked of superiority.

My response was classic. "I am not angry!" I shot back.

"Yes, you are. You're an angry woman."

I wanted to wring his neck! The nerve of that twit! How dare this worldly, image-conscious, pagan shampooer of heads, this terrible, macho, tacky, quasi artiste, accuse me—a Christian, wife of a minister, Sunday school teacher, and seeker of things spiritual—of something so ugly as being an angry woman!

Who did he think he was? What did he know about issues of the soul?

Trevor glowed with self-satisfaction. He knew by my response that he had hit a nerve. With perverse ease he had read my soul, found my fissure, and let me know I had no reason to feel superior. He knew that spiritual people should not also be angry people, and he knew I knew it too. How he enjoyed holding the mirror to my soul to my face and showing me what I did not want to see.

It was the changing-room experience all over again. What a surprise that a worldly man would have such spiritual perception! I honestly had not noticed that anger last swimsuit season. I was shocked. Trevor the Terrible, tacky quasi artiste, macho chain-puller of women, had just done the colors of Valerie Bell's soul!

Was I an angry woman? My emotional response indicated that I was either insulted at Trevor's nerve or that he had hit a nerve. Was he on to something? Was anger becoming an obvious part of my lifestyle? Surely he was just trying to get a reaction from me.

It was the first alarming hint that my soul might not be aging well. I was barely thirty-something, and if Trevor was right, I was on my way to becoming "one of *those* kinds" of old people.

Please Tell Me I'm Not Becoming "One of Those Kinds" of Old People

It's amazing how memorable poorly-aged people are. Our encounters with them may be brief, but they can be nasty enough to make us think we actually have bumped into a soul turned toxic dump site.

I encountered an old bully in the grocery store one stormy, wintry night. Most sensible folks managed to stay home out of the blustery weather, but against my better judgment, I weathered the snowy cold for some necessary food staple—at least something my sons felt they could not live without. My car was one of only five in the unplowed lot.

The old man approached me at the check-cashing station inside. In a booming voice calculated to attract attention, he barked, "'S that your Honda, lady?

"Yes," I answered, glancing at the lot and back again at the towering, flush-faced old crank.

"Well, you're illegally parked! That's a handicapped spot and there's no handicapped sticker on your car!" His words were full of disdain.

Thinking we were discussing a moot point since undoubtedly the lot would remain vacant that night, I checked again. No, I had parked *next* to a handicapped space. I avoid handicapped spaces with near religiosity. Even though the blizzard made it impossible to distinguish the lines, this was my regular store; I knew my spaces!

"Oh, I'm sorry. You're mistaken. That's a regular space," I answered, feeling assured that graciousness would clear up the misunderstanding and appease my accuser.

"GO TO #$&*, LADY!" he spat. "YOU MAKE ME SICK! I OUGHT TO CALL THE POLICE ON YOU!"

He crushed me like a bug. I was stunned and humiliated by his loud, public attack.

He, however, turned to sashay down the baked goods' aisle with an obviously pleased-with-himself gait. He spoke jovially to the stock boys. He was expansive and jocular and friendly. The opportunity to bully someone had apparently made this miserable old misanthrope's night.

Someone should let the hot air out of his ego-sized balloon! I thought.

I remembered reading a quote (whose source is unfortunately lost to me now) that said, "An angry middle-aged person is usually a jerk." This angry man was older than middle-aged. He had probably marinated in his anger for seven or more decades. He was beyond jerk. As much as I disliked him, I also recognized my uncared-for soul's potential in that man.

Jerkiness is definitely not reserved for the male of the species. Once again, that great laboratory of life, the grocery store, would be my schoolroom for human character development—feminine style. It was a busy day. The store was packed. The customer service counter at the office (for people needing special help with returns, exchanges, rain checks, and questions about out-of-stock products) was jammed and moving as slow as grandma's garters. Shopping carts pointed in every direction. Lines were nonexistent. There seemed to be no system for keeping order. We were all on our honor, depending on each other's manners and courtesy to find our eventual place to the front. I dutifully took a spot at the back of the bulge, behind everyone who was there before me. Mothers in front of me coped with fussy toddlers and babies. No one exchanged chitchat. For fifteen minutes we seemed to be at a dead stop. While we all quietly endured this frustration, I amused myself by making faces at babies, trying to make them smile. I did wide eyes, shifty eyes, and fish faces, making a public fool of myself to pass the time. Then, from the corner of my eye, I watched as an old woman joined the group. She made no attempt to find her place behind the others. Quickly and stealthily, she worked her way around the edge. Unencumbered by shopping cart or children, she went almost immediately to the front of the group. This was no bag lady. She was dressed stylishly in a sequined jogging suit, matching hat, and tennies. I was flabbergasted when the clerk asked, "Who's next?" and this sequined old babe raised her hand and pushed ahead of everyone else. There was no way she was next. Even the clerk knew it. Everyone exchanged "can-you-believe-her-nerve!" glances, but no one raised a complaint.

Too bad we were not all back in kindergarten. Then our hands would have waved wildly at our teacher, our voices demanding justice, whining that a great travesty had been committed. Someone had not waited her turn! Someone had butted in line! Instead, we resisted the urge to act like children ourselves. We sighed. We waited. We rolled our eyes at each other. We deferred to her age and hoped we would not have to be nice to any other oldsters that day.

Beware of Soul Traps

What kind of future can an angry thirty-something woman anticipate? If Trevor were right, my future probably held only a few bleak alternatives. The first possibility would find me becoming less and less able, or willing even, to hide my poisonous anger from other people. In time, more and more people would see me as an angry woman. In time, anger would destroy all my relationships. The second alternative would be to fake it, to have an exterior all-is-well front that hid the really angry woman from view as much as possible. Either way anger would dwell just slightly beneath the surface, waiting to spring.

I might become like my unattractive grocery-store oldsters. They illustrate one of the major negative inclinations of the untended aging soul: a growing tendency to care less about what other people think or feel. It's as if the editing mechanism on human interaction breaks down—the monitor on appropriateness and kindness stops working. For many, aging is an excuse to shed societal propriety. We become naughty, even cruel children in wrinkled bodies. In *Having Our Say: The Delany Sisters' First 100 Years* Bessie Delany put it this way, "When you get real old, honey, you realize there are certain things that just don't matter anymore. You lay it all on the table. There's a saying: Only little children and old folks tell the truth."[1]

Unfortunately, while "laying it all on the table" and behaving as if certain things do not matter has an appeal, it is often practiced at the expense of other people. Anger, combined with a weakening sense of social propriety, is great potential for human toxic dump site development. "Anger is a sin against the gift of social life; anger has no neighbors, only enemies and obstacles."[2]

Most people develop a more subtle approach to their aging character than "laying it all on the table." We care mostly about how we are perceived, not who we are actually becoming. We allow a widening gap to develop between our packaging and our true character. We are marked by inconsistencies; our smiles cover our hostility; our words hide our true intentions; politeness and social niceties mark our human exchanges—but inside we are feeling the opposite. We are not what we appear to be. This approach to aging could be characterized as "What you see is not what you get."

This was the approach of a certain Mrs. Congeniality from a recent state beauty pageant. "She was someone you would like to have back every year," said the executive director of the pageant. "She was very popular. . . . She's a great lady, friendly, congenial, a person ready to cooperate at every turn." But according to her neighbors back home, she was far from "Mrs. Congeniality." They cite a school board meeting when she slapped a police officer who disagreed with her. Then there was the more serious incident pending in court over a time when, while driving a car, she supposedly tried to run over a neighbor's child. Mrs. Congeniality's response to her neighbors' accusations? "That's not me. I know who I am and the person I am."3 Presumably, she thinks she's a congenial woman.

Hmm. What's happening here? Who could have guessed? It's that evil twin syndrome. Mrs. Congeniality probably has an evil twin who runs around her neighborhood, impersonates her, and destroys her reputation. It sounds as though it could be the plot of a soap opera. The evil twin theory explains a lot in life actually. Maybe many of us have evil twins, saying nasty things, behaving boorishly, and confusing people—even confusing ourselves about who we really are.

Come on. The public feedback suggests Mrs. Congeniality is both a woman who can be extremely charming and also a woman who can be extremely nasty. The mirror reflecting her soul's progression suggests she may not be in touch with who she really is becoming. Scary!

The evil twin. Inconsistencies of the soul. We are so skilled at being out of touch with our soul's progression. Have you noticed any of these perverse skills developing in your life: The ability to turn the charm off and on when it benefits you? To be wonderfully friendly when it serves your purposes? To be selectively polite to the right people? To seem cooperative at beneficial moments but in reality (when the spotlight is turned off or especially when the heat is turned up) to turn nasty? If so, your Evil Twin may be on the loose.

Scripture has a phrase for such an approach: cup polishing. Interestingly, some of the strongest words of Jesus were directed at this human tendency to develop a gap between our public packaging and our true selves, to indulge in personal image-making, to be inconsistent in our character. Notice Jesus' words spoken to those who consider themselves religious but whose tendency was to be more concerned with their public image than with their inner reality. Notice the intensity, the edge of disdain: "Woe to you, Pharisees, and you religious leaders—hypocrites! You are so careful to polish the outside of the cup, but the inside is foul with extortion and greed. Blind Pharisees! First cleanse the inside of the cup, and then the whole cup will be clean" (Matthew 23: 25–26 TLB).

Jesus' strong rebuke addresses the subtle approach to aging and character development taken by many, this tendency of letting a gap develop between our image—our public persona—and our soul—our inner reality, our intrinsic self.

Where Is the Food and Drug Administration When We Need It?

Supermarket encounters with such poorly cared-for souls makes me think that what is missing in life is a system to protect ourselves from each other. We need labels. Prominent ones. Obvious ones. The Food and Drug Administration could print content labels for people as they do for food. After all, a one-time encounter with the most fat-laden, calorie-soaked food can't begin to damage us like a one-time encounter with an ugly soul. Quickly we could look past each other's packaging to the Character Facts and see one another's true character. There before our very eyes by descending prominence would be displayed the characteristics of a person's soul. Anger would top the list of the old man who slimed me. If he had been labeled, I would have been able to take some comfort that our encounter was probably not unique to me. I could have ducked. Self-centeredness would be the primary content on the label of the sequined old babe. Outbursts of anger would top the list for "Mrs. Congeniality." Character Facts. I like it.

Jerk Potential

"The older the violin," the letters on the pillow in the gift shop declare, *"the sweeter the music!"* Would it were so with adults as well. Unfortunately, for most people, getting sweeter is the exception, not the rule.

While we sympathize with the trials of aging to a point, we also hold a particular disdain for older persons who have not managed to get their act together. A self-centered, older woman droning on about her failing health is difficult to admire. The older person who could care less about what other people think, who operates with an obviously receding moral force, seems particularly distasteful, as is an old cup polisher whose public image is nothing but an attempt to hide a nasty inner reality and manipulate others. What about the aging, angry woman who acts spiritually superior? She is as hard to swallow as any other version of the obnoxious older person. What about the character you are becoming? How potentially repulsive is the untended, aging soul!

While angry young men and women sometimes manage to change the world, I see the truth in the hard statement, "An angry middle-aged person is usually a jerk." The pain of youth (which can be motivating) when left to smolder and grow into a lifestyle of unchecked middle-aged anger or bitterness or self-pity, is ground in which full-fledged jerkiness can take root. While terms such as *old coot, geezer, codger, old crock, grannies,* and *biddies* may reflect ageism at its worst, if we are blatantly honest, we probably know a few middle-agers who have begun earning such derogatory titles.

What had happened in the lives of my grocery-store characters to turn them repulsive in their older years? What was occurring in the life of a woman who could be the champion of congeniality for a week and the neighborhood jerk the rest of the time? What was happening to me? Do we begin life as angry people or self-centered bullies who care little about what others think of them? When do we start feeling comfortable with gaps between our souls and our images? Poor soul development is a process. It may begin as early as childhood with a first heartbreak, a major rejection, an emotional abandonment, a great injustice, or an abuse of some kind. Experts advise us that character development begins a long time before the age of sixty-five. Soul development, be it poor or exceptionally fine, begins early in life.

Whether you are twenty or thirty or fifty, you have already invested either negatively or positively in your soul's development. It's fairly easy to tell how your soul is progressing. Have you taken on some negative characteristics, some nasty personality traits you did not have as a child or as a teenager? Have you noticed a tendency to be less interested in others now or more prone to outbursts of anger? Have you caught yourself bullying or intimidating a salesperson or telemarketer? Do children bother you a lot? Have you gotten any negative feedback, cues about your soul's development lately? What if Charles Dickens wrote about your life and you were the one visited by the Ghost of Christmas Past? Would such an apparition remind you that in earlier days you were a sweeter, kinder, generally better person than you are today? Have the changes in your life through the years been positive or negative? What emotions have you made a part of your lifestyle? Have you protected and guarded your soul? Or would an honest description of you reveal that you are a hostile, caustic, aging person?

The well-tended soul weeds out what is ugly and malignant and false. Not only is there a weeding process, but there is a purposeful building into the soul the things that are beautiful and worthy and redemptive.

When Provokers Give Painful Gifts

Having someone label me as an angry woman was extremely embarrassing. I had been careful to be Mrs. Congeniality with most people, but Trevor had uncovered the duplicity of such cup polishing. How ironic that a professional cup polisher—a body beautician—had read my soul! It was a red flag. How would I respond? Defensively? Would I cover my ears and write him off? Or could I entertain the possibility that what Trevor had said had actually been a gift to help me develop my intrinsic self? Was there some wisdom in listening to the man?

His assessment hadn't felt friendly and constructive. I think he was a provoker—someone who probably did not really have my best interests in mind. Like most provokers, he has a gift of reading others at their lowest possible interpretation. Such provokers can actually enjoy the pain they cause.

And yet provokers serve a purpose in life. Particularly if we are interested in developing well, provokers can help us in their own perverse way. They hold up mirrors to our souls and point out the ugliness inside. In my case, I wondered if "Only my hairdresser knows for sure" was a true statement. I wondered who else had encountered me and been left with the impression that I was an angry woman.

More and More the Real Woman Emerges

With each passing year, you and I have an increased potential for seeing the real woman inside. A progressively wrinkled body is an invitation to discover the real you. It is an opportunity to shift focus from that which is mortal to that which is eternal. This shift can be viewed not so much as a loss but as an opportunity to cultivate depth and connectedness and soulfulness. One author expressed it this way:

> Aging brings out the flavors of a personality. The individual emerges over time, the way fruit matures and ripens. In the Renaissance view, depression, aging, and individuality all go together: the sadness of growing old is part of becoming an individual. Melancholy thoughts carve out an interior space where wisdom can take up residence.[4]

Looking in the mirror of my soul and seeing a potentially angry woman staring back was enlightening. Continued unchecked, I could imagine myself as I aged. There I was, yelling at a young man in the grocery store for parking in a handicapped space. There I was as a wrinkled old babe in a sequined sweatsuit edging my way to the front of the line, butting ahead of the young women with babies because my time was so much more important than anyone else's. There I was—scolding the postal carrier for delivering my mail late, bawling out the paper boy for terrorizing my tulips, screaming at children for walking on my grass, slapping a policeman, gunning my car accelerator to clear the children from the street. Without a soul adjustment, it was all just a matter of time before such possibilities became reality.

Where can a person go for "nice" lessons? Can graciousness be learned? Could I reverse my aging tendencies and become sweeter? Would I heal enough to stop not only the bleeding but the anger as well? I needed a map to help me put together the pieces of my journey for the days to come. Maybe I would not just grow old. Perhaps I would make, with some divine help, a spiritual quest of this journey.

I came home from the salon that day ready to pose the question, "I'm not an angry woman, am I?" to my husband. I was brimming with "Can you believe it?" I wanted validation that this confrontation had been all Trevor's fault. Steve was reassuring. He said I was incredibly easy to live with. "Angry? I never think of you that way!" he laughed.

Here is the strange part of my story: My husband, who loves me, was not a good mirror for my soul. He simply loved me too well to notice those growing tendencies I was even unwilling to admit to myself. He probably justified my poor disposition as grief.

I realized it started that way, but that I had learned a more aggressive emotion that made me feel less like a victim. I was angry at life. I was angry with God. I felt God had let me down in the early deaths of my parents. Even the small crumb of saying good-bye to each of them had been denied. It wasn't right! It wasn't fair! Now, years after their deaths my wounds were no longer bleeding; I had discovered anger and had covered my wounds with anger's calluses. Anger made me feel more in charge, less vulnerable, less passive. Anger felt so much better than pain. Those feelings were with me always, just under the surface. I hadn't even seen it myself! Trevor had shown me the truth. For the first time, I faced my stiffness, my impatience, my smoldering. Oh, how I hated to admit it! That infuriating pagan hairdresser was right. *O God*, I prayed, *how did my life ever become this disordered?*

In *Disordered Lives: Healing the Seven Deadly Sins*, William S. Stafford examines anger that becomes sinful.

> Feelings of anger, like any other strong feelings, may be right in origin, yet go wrong so easily. Anger can become a permanent part of the character of a person or a nation, a disposition always ready to move into action. In sinful anger, the "irritable" response turns around a basically selfish set of assumptions about reality. The standard is set by our own determination of what is normal and right. Deciding what is right is not left to God or anyone else. . . . Individuals or whole peoples can gnaw at old grievances, remembering them again and again, renewing them obsessively until the shape of memory and desire is permanently warped along the lines of anger. Life itself is shaped by anger; one's self is defined by anger. Few things are as terrible as knowing an old man or old woman whose personality would collapse if it were not held rigid by resentment.[5]

Few things, that is, except knowing *you* are becoming that old, angry woman! Trevor had uncovered a truth about my becoming. I realized that I could no longer ignore the development of my soul. I was alarmed at what Trevor had shown me in my soul mirror. My soul was fitting itself to anger, forming in character to the dimensions of every repulsive, angry person I had ever known. Anger was becoming a permanent part of my character.

It was time to weed anger out of my life. I discovered the inappropriateness of my anger at God. I looked behind the anger at my pain. This woundedness would need healing, not just a callous covering of the anger. It was time to recover my softness and gentleness. Time to learn to laugh again (and in my case learn to cry when I was hurt). My soul needed a makeover. It was time to end the Protestant nun stage of my life. I began to drape my soul in lighter hues, sweeter shades. My encounter with Trevor began a process of shaping my soul to God's dimensions, not anger's.

A Thank-You to Trevor

Looking back, I realize Trevor did me a tremendous favor. When I think of all the benefits in my life that came from my encounter with him, I have thought that I should drop him a note—thanking him, admitting that he was right about me.

Dear Trevor, (it would begin)

> You may not remember me. I used to come to your salon, excuse me, studio. I was the woman who wore the wrong colors—the one who told you she dressed for her soul. I'm sure that sounded really spiritually superior to you. I was a young minister's wife. Still can't remember me? Okay. Try this. The angry one?
>
> (I imagine that would bring a smile to his face.)
>
> I never came back to your shop. I was too embarrassed to let you know that you were right about me. That's because you did more than my hair. You 'did my colors' on several levels, Trevor.
>
> What I want to say is I know you told me I was angry to take me down a peg. And you did. But you also did

something else. You helped me to see myself as others might. I've done some soul-searching since then. Actually made some major adjustments. I think you would notice some changes in me.

Oh, I still wear all the wrong colors—some of us are just dense that way, you know. But since our conversation, or shall I say confrontation, I'm less tense, quicker to smile, less prone to pass judgment for small things.

I'm not bragging; I realize that I still have some work to do in this area, but I want to operate within the realm of grace that recognizes that what is intended to wound us can, with God's help, actually bring about great good in our lives. Thanks for doing my 'spiritual' colors.

Yours truly,
Valerie Bell

P.S. Has the women's movement impacted your town yet, or is your salon, excuse me, studio, still full? Sorry, couldn't resist. After all, I'm not perfect, just working on improving!

Three

Soul Goals

*The great danger facing all of us . . . is not that we shall
make an absolute failure of life, nor that we shall fall into
outright viciousness, nor that we shall be terribly unhappy,
nor that we shall feel that life has no meaning at all—not
these things. The danger is that we may fail to perceive life's
greatest meaning, fall short of its highest good, miss its deepest and most abiding happiness, be unable to render the
most needed service, be unconscious of life ablaze with the
light of the Presence of God—and be content to have it
so—that is the danger. . . . That is what one prays one's
friends may be spared—satisfaction with life that falls short
of the best.*

—Phillip Brooks

$\mathcal{W}$hen I was young, I had such puny goals for my life. While
still in college I married, quite purposefully, a fellow student who
told me his life's goal was to become a medical doctor. In Bible
college I avoided the young men who received ministry calls to
places like Inner Zambia and Outer Mongolia. *Nice guy!* I would
think. *But better to stay away from someone headed in that direction!* I took a second look at Steve Bell—and he at me. He was

47

so much fun. I could not imagine him involved in something so intense as ministry! It seemed like a perfect match.

My mother thought differently. She had conceived and birthed all three of her children with difficulty, under Hannah-like circumstances. Like Hannah's miracle child, Samuel, we had all been given back to God for full-time Christian service. It was the promise she had made. She intended that we would keep her end of the bargain!

My mother-in-law even reports that in one of their first conversations, my mother very clearly stated that she hoped Steve was going into the ministry, if we intended to be married. As far as Mother was concerned, I had already been promised and called into such work.

I was a reluctant Samuel. My parents' home was ministry humble. My father was a music professor at a Bible college. Money was short. I thought we suffered from a kind of "quality of life" deprivation. I was looking for a change from what I termed "temple life." Being married to someone whose occupation promised such bright prospects for life security was a definite part of my attraction to Steve. I dreamed about spending my life sipping lemonade by a pool (my twenty-year-old misconception of how doctors' wives spent their lives!). Soon, however, after only one year of marriage with another year of college yet to go, Steve broke the news to me: His goals were changing. He felt God was calling him into the ministry. Would I support his changed plans? Suddenly his changed plans were seriously impacting my goals for the future. It could make a young woman wonder if marrying under false pretenses is grounds for divorce. My fond dreams of sipping lemonade by a pool and living my life as a kept woman began to slip away from me.

I managed to say yes to my young husband's ministry call. My mother was thrilled. Now all three of her children had entered the ministry. It was not an entirely happy time for me, however. Deep inside I thought I was saying good-bye to owning a home or wearing clothes purchased at places other than second-hand stores. I would never travel. I resigned myself to working to supplement the family income; I would do some of my own keeping. I sorrowfully abandoned my own dreams, one by one. Undoubtedly we would be church-mouse poor, and I would never see the world. I would lead a provincial and boring life!

We have been married for twenty-six years now and most of those years have been ministry years. For nine years Steve was a pastor. Then we joined the staff of The Chapel of the Air radio broadcast for twelve years, and for the past few years he has served as executive director of Concerts of Prayer International while I have been speaking and writing. Looking back, I am so grateful God intervened in our life's goals. My gifts are ministry gifts, and I am most happy when I am using them. A life by a pool might have been a real frustration for someone like me. At twenty-something I didn't know myself well enough to plan the best for the days to come. I planned for security. Fortunately, God planned for growth. Ministry has been rewarding, personally stretching, a backdrop for growth on multiple levels, and surprisingly fulfilling! My plans, in retrospect, are the ones that seemed provincial and boring!

Several years into our marriage and ministry, I nearly tasted the irony of my puny plans and God's intervention as I drank in the experience of being in Machu Picchu, the Lost City of the Incas. I, who had avoided Inner Mongolia and Outer Zambia, now found myself, along with my husband, leading a student missionary trip that brought us to the Andes Mountains of Peru, as well as to many other countries during our life together. How thrilling to meet believers of another culture! What a great experience to serve these children of God, to participate in their lives, to worship together, if only for a brief time. I was so inspired by everything I experienced overseas. I never could have anticipated during my college years that missions would fascinate me in the least. It occurred to me during that trip all I would have missed if I had settled for a more calculated, secure material plan!

With the awareness of God's goodness in our lives, we experienced a plane ride into Cuzco, the ancient capital of the Inca empire. History shone from the Incan stonework that formed the foundation for the conquering Spanish and their European-styled, brick cathedrals. After a night in a hotel, allowing our bodies some time to adjust to the mountain air, we experienced a faltering, jerky train ride deep into the mountains and a hairpin, nerve-wracking bus ride up Machu Picchu, a 7,480-foot mountain. Pinch yourself, Valerie Bell! Even in my wildest dreams, I had never imagined myself standing in the middle of the remains of a beautiful and mysterious ancient Incan city. This was a far cry from lemonade by a pool, girl!

Our students quickly acclimated to the rare air, clambering over the ruins of boulder-puzzle temples and verdant terraces like hearty, young mountain goats. Our guide informed us that, to this day, no one knows how the Indians were able to haul such huge boulders to their mountaintop building site. Nor could scientists explain how the Incas were able to fit the boulders so snugly that even the edge of a razor blade could not fit through the cracks! High above the Urubamba River this ancient city nests a home for condors, who glide through the sky above. It is magic and mystery and wonder, a sight of a lifetime! A dream come true despite my fear of unrealized expectations.

But I will never forget the man we met as we came down from that mountain. Along the side of the path we said hello to a sixty-something-year-old man sitting alone at the base of the ruins. He asked us about the view from the top. Was it as beautiful as all the pictures he had seen, he wondered? His question puzzled us. Why was he asking us? He was only several hundred yards (all up steep steps) from one of the most beautiful sights on earth!

Then he told us his story. I still remember his words: "You kids are really doing this right. I traveled all through Europe when I was younger, and now I've come all this way to see this historic wonder, but I can't go any further! The walk to the top is too strenuous. The air is too thin. My heart is too weak. I didn't plan my travel well for my old age. What a shame!"

Imagine. He was so close to one of the most magnificent experiences of his life. But sadly, he would not fully enjoy Machu Picchu that day, or likely ever. He had failed to plan for the limitations of aging. His plans could have been better. His words were filled with regret.

The Importance of Planning

That man's dilemma impressed me that day, almost as much as the ruins. It made me realize that aging well takes some planning. It's so easy to lose focus, fail to stretch for the best life has to offer, and end life full of regrets.

Several months after my fortieth birthday, I was reading about establishing lifetime goals. The author suggested making a list of twenty-five things you want to experience before you die. Dream a little, plan a little was the suggestion. This list was to be tucked into your wallet and referred to often.[1]

Remembering the older man at Machu Picchu, I recognized this as an excellent suggestion. I went to my favorite room in my home, my sunny bedroom. I took the phone off the hook and for the next hour, I planned a little for the days to come. I let my heart lead and refused my head permission to edit my dreams. Here's part of that list:

Before I die I want to . . .

Get into good physical shape. Lose that extra ten, okay fifteen, pounds sometime before I die. Increase my energy and sense of well-being through exercise. Take my medicine regularly. Learn not to feel guilty about caring for myself. If I splurge for a manicure, for instance, I will give myself permission to enjoy it rather than feeling guilty about the time and money.

Improve my cooking. Learn more low-fat cooking techniques. Eat well. Eat out less. Entertain more often.

Sing duets with my teenage son, Justin (who will probably hate this idea!).

Travel. Especially spend an extended time in a French-speaking country so I can use the six years of French I had in school. Maybe even write about my impressions as in *A Year in Provence.*

Weed out my closet. Buy classics and accessorize.

Live on a lake or near water.

Become proficient and knowledgeable in prayer.

Learn more about gardening.

Build a special house.

In that vein, my list continued. I tucked it away in my devotional Bible. Occasionally, I looked at it. But something bothered me about this list. It seemed incomplete, as if something important was missing. Actually, I began to think that this whole approach seemed a little skewed. The instructions had said, ". . . before you die." That was what disturbed me!

For the most part, my list had a clinging-to-this-world feeling. My goals seemed not only extremely domestic and centered on my family, but temporal as well. They reminded me of some other provincial and boring plans I had made for my life when I was younger.

Did any of my goals take into account my inner person, my soul? Goals for the development of my mind were on my list. Goals that I thought would improve the quality of my life in other ways were on that list, but many of them were material. Where was the care of my soul in my plans for the future? Would a sparkling new house on a lake necessarily improve my life in any way? Many unhappy people live in sparkling houses on lakes, after all. Their good fortune sometimes further isolates them from other people instead of increasing their connectedness. Gardening would increase the quality of my life, but already my hands are beginning to feel the pain of arthritis; in time I would have to give it up anyway. An organized wardrobe would make me feel more "together" until next year when the styles all changed or if I gained weight, making my closet obsolete. Learning French might be good for my intellect, but a soul can ache in any language.

I examined this list that had inadvertently exposed my values. Was this what I wanted in life? The goals that I thought would make my life more "soulish" had actually diverted me and left my soul basically uncared for. As carefully as I had begun the process of weeding out anger's grip in my life, I now realized I must just as carefully build in the things that would increase my sense of well-being, my happiness, my higher fulfillment, my spiritual joy, my sense of connectedness with God and others, and a tenacious inner strength that would see me through "before I die."

I reexamined my list. Would any of these dreams I held so dear travel well with my soul into eternity? No, I had to admit.

Most of my goals were earthbound; there was not a sense of the days to come, which would include eternity. Most of my values were limited to this life.

The problem with dreams and goals of an earthly dimension is they are not big enough for our souls. I was amazed at the smallness of my dreams. I might as well have stated my goals for the second half of my life right alongside that famous eccentric woman whose objective in her aging was mostly the shedding of societal propriety. The title of her poem became the title of a best-selling book: *When I Am Old I Shall Wear Purple.* Judging from the popularity of that poem—on T-shirts, posters, greeting cards—the idea of aging without regard for societal restraints appeals to a lot of us. The poet—whose plans for her aging included shocking the public with spitting, the wearing of red with purple, the picking of flowers from other people's gardens, and the shedding of her youthful sobriety—and I were soul sisters. We both planned small for the days ahead. Neither of our "before I die" plans would greatly impact our own lives or the world at large.

Valerie Bell, I chastised myself, *haven't you grown up at all in these past twenty-five years? You know you were born for more than preparing healthy cuisine and speaking French! Are you really satisfied just to breathe air and sip gourmet lemonade by the pool in your wrinkled skin and purple and red swimsuit? If all these dreams came to pass, would you really be happy—soul happy?*

Do Your Dreams Reflect Spiritual Values?

Where was the spiritual quest in my journey toward and beyond "before I die"? Was a deep spirituality a reality to me? I thought it was, but why then wasn't it reflected more strongly in my values? Plan a life that overlooks the development of the soul and the outcome is sure to be disappointing. What were my *soul goals*, my higher dreams?

The words of Scripture seem appropriately helpful in my struggle to gain a perspective on life with the soul's development in mind.

> Therefore we do not lose heart. Though outwardly we are wasting away, yet inwardly we are being renewed day by day. . . . So we fix our eyes not on what is seen, but on what is unseen. For what is seen is temporary, but what is unseen is eternal (2 Corinthians 4:16, 18).

I needed another set of plans, one that nurtured the renewal of my soul, my intrinsic self. I needed goals that would fix my eyes on inner realities. A commitment to inner development is the defining element to quality living. As my body wastes away, I need to sense my soul is increasingly strengthening, improving, counterbalancing whatever loss I may be experiencing with age.

Again, words of Scripture, this time warning the eternal soul of the danger of having only earthly dreams, "Though he was always greedy, now he has nothing; of all the things he dreamed of—none remain" (Job 20:20 TLB).

Revising the Dream List

Which of my dreams will remain? Perhaps the important question to ask ourselves is not just, "What twenty-five things do I want to experience *before I die?*" But, "What twenty-five things do I want to have impacted *because I lived?*"

Sixty-five years of age is too old to begin thinking about the long-range future. By then, the untended soul has piled up regrets, bitterness, and orneriness of all kinds. It will have become as weak as the body it dwells in. Now is the time to strengthen the soul for the journey into the future. Go ahead. Plan for excellence on every level—materially, relationally, physically—but don't forget to plan excellence for your soul as well.

Dreams Big Enough for Your Soul

What is a soul goal? It is a goal that positions us for the very best life has to offer: real contentment, instead of the restlessness of soul that drives many women to keep moving, redecorating, acquiring better things; deep joy that is evident in the midst of any life circumstance, good or bad; a growing relationship with God that leads to inner peace and a profound sense of well-being; a deeper commitment to others that connects our souls to them at the most intimate level. Only a well-cared-for soul can deliver those goods. Looking at my original list of "before I die " goals, I realized that I was making a common mistake. All my goals were attempts at more "soulish" living, but they could not produce the qualities of life I really desired. I kept the original list. The dreams listed there are not wrong, but they are incomplete. I added some soul goals to my dreams. Here they are:

1. *I want to delight God.* Scriptures say that God's eyes scan the earth searching for those whose hearts are right toward him. I desire to be one of those with whom he can consistently find comfort and pleasure. I want to "make his day" as Noah did. Even in a dark day, God found pleasure in Noah. That is the kind of relationship I want with God. I want him to find comfort with me and experience delight when he thinks about me. I want to learn to hear God's holy laughter regarding me. I want that delight in life that only an open, intimate relationship with God can give.

2. *I want to "practice heaven" by enjoying God now.* The *Westminster Catechism* declares that the chief end of humankind

is to glorify God and enjoy him forever. I want to experience the pleasure of knowing God with greater intensity as I age. I want my soul to become skilled and comfortable in the practice of heaven—praising and enjoying God. I'm acclimating my eternal soul, my intrinsic self, to the values of heaven now.

3. *I want to have a part in advancing God's kingdom.* Nothing would please me more than knowing I had seriously thwarted the destructive plans of the Evil One. I want there to be no doubt about which side benefited from my loyalties. Understand, I am not envisioning some kind of Joan of Arc role here. I am not wanting to be grandiose or spiritually ambitious. But I want to be increasingly available and skilled for the part God might want me to play in his holy drama.

4. *I want to remain open to the unexpected, off-the-beaten-path plans of God for my life.* I intend to nurture an adventuresome spirit. Why not be open to things in my sixties that I would not consider at a younger age? Forget the small shockers like spitting and picking flowers from other people's gardens. I want to drape my soul in purple and be open to experiencing mission work in Kenya at sixty or a house filled with children at seventy. I want to develop an eagerness for the unconventional, pathless-traveled life. I am not motivated by the shock appeal, however, but by the awareness that God can use people whose boundaries with him are unconventional and well off the beaten path.

5. *I want to grow in loving graciousness in my relationships.* I want to mellow toward others as I age. I want to be remembered as a truly loving person, not a tough, old bird! I would like to become more of a safe place for the people in my life. I would like my connections with others to be increasingly marked by compassion and an ability to connect with others soul to soul.

6. *I want to laugh more.* I just like the way a laugh rings in the face of evil. There is a holy craziness to an aging woman who can still laugh. "I have confidence in God!" is what that kind of laughter communicates. I love that!

7. *I want to think less like a victim and more like a survivor.* I have some significant life wounds by this point. Don't we all? But I want to feel that I have done more than suffered with these pains. I want to know that I have turned them into learning experiences, builders of interior character. I want to experience "beauty for ashes" as I review the unfolding of my life. May my life deepen, not wither because of painful life experiences.

8. *I want to reaffirm my desire to excel in prayer!* I want my aging to be impacted by contact and communion with God. May I become more astute at hearing God's voice and seeing things, not just from a human perspective but from God's perspective.

The picture of the soul these goals capture is a soul that is intimate with God. It is not an ominous relationship, marked by heaving sighs and flowing tears, but one characterized by mutual delight. The soul is relaxed, open, flexible, full of joy, and ready to connect deeply on many relational levels.

Before and After Soul

The heart of my goals is not to have the soul of my fortieth birthday. Then my soul was marked by anxiety and shattered trust concerning God's intentions for my future. My forty-year-old soul was afraid of life. The soul of my goals today points 180 degrees in the opposite direction. This soul embraces life.

Shortly after my cancer diagnosis, the prescription for strengthening my health inadvertently opened the door to new healing for my soul as well. "Walk," my doctor had written on her prescription pad, "five times a week, forty minutes a day." At first it appeared to be a frustrating commitment of time, but eventually I found a way to make it ultimately productive. I could walk for my soul as well as for my body. I began to pray as I walked. I talked for a while, and then I would listen. That was my introduction to "prayerwalking." One of the early comforts God gave me was the reassurance that my life was not out of control. "Valerie, you will live as long as intended by my will. Not a day more. Not a day less." What a relief. It was as if my soul let out a deep sigh and then relaxed. I did not need to feel any responsibility about the timing of my body wearing out. God was in charge. I was in his perfect will. I could trust God with my life one day at a time.

Step-by-tep, day in and day out, five times a week for forty minutes a day, I began to have a renewed sense of the wonder of life and fell in love with living again. Prayer taught me that even though I was a woman with cancer, God had been good to me just the same. Cancer did not alter the fact that my life had been blessed. I began to feel grateful for the multitude sweetnesses of life: my family, my friends, my home, and joys previously taken for granted.

I was beginning to heal on a deeply spiritual level. Where had this delight in God come from? It was as if we shared our little jokes and at times I found myself singing or laughing right out loud. A deep comfort held me, and my soul lightened and sweetened in response. Interestingly, my life postcancer was marked by a quality of living I had not experienced before. For me, oddly enough, cancer turned out to be a kind of mixed blessing.

How Will Your Life Be Summarized?

It is a gift to realize early on that the days to come will include a day of laying down life to death. Why a gift? Because the days before that final day become more precious. The days that lie between here and that final day become invested and more committed to quality living on every level. When I think of the end now, I think of it very differently. I think of packing in as much love and joy and caring as possible. I know a brush with the reality of death has made me more intentional in my living. I am more highly aware of what I really want from life. When I die, the obituary will probably be pretty ordinary. A small blurb may announce something like this:

> Valerie Burton Bell, 87, a Chicago writer and speaker, died Sunday at DuPage Medical Center. Mrs. Bell was born in Chicago. She is survived by her husband, Steve, and two sons, Brendan and Justin, and ten grandchildren.

That's how earth may observe my passing. But in heaven I'm hoping my arrival will read in some "Heavenly Herald" more like this:

> Valerie Burton Bell entered eternal life Sunday. She died while on a tour of missionary outposts in Zambia and Mongolia. She was an unusually wrinkled eighty-seven-year-old woman and will be very happy with her new, improved body. On earth her writing and speaking expressed a strong desire to be a woman who delighted in walking with God. She started a little weak but improved as she matured. People who knew her often remarked that even as her body slowed and bent, she seemed increasingly lively as if she were "younging." Welcome to heaven a woman who is a friend of God's. You will recognize her by her laugh.

Will any of these things ever be said of me? I am almost embarrassed to articulate such thoughts because I realize how far I am from my ideal. But it is the course I have set for my soul.

How about you? Do you have dreams for your soul? Do any of your life goals include those for your interior self? Do you have a clear picture of the woman you hope to become? Do you understand that you are being formed for eternity now?

Join me. Look forward with me to the rarefied air of heaven, where we will no longer "see through a glass darkly" but will have perfect spiritual perception, where our souls will clamber through heaven acclimatized to God through well-lived years on earth. Far better to experience aging, not so much as a grieving and letting go of earthly joys but as soul strengthening that improves life on every level. Aging is a training period for the ultimate joy of coming home to an infinitely better life.

I'm learning to gain perspective on my aging by keeping the bigger picture in sight. These middle years have convinced me that it's critically important to foster a spiritual outlook, to loosen gradually my hold on things that are temporary and prone to decay while I learn to operate more easily in the areas belonging to my spirit. *The greatest mistake in aging is not simply failing to plan but failing to plan for the very best.*

Wanting More!

Honestly, I would still like to build a house someday or live in France for a period of time. Lemonade still tastes delicious. I am not throwing away those earthly pleasures. I just realize that in the area of my heart where I hold my treasures, those dreams are not all I want. I want more! The bigger spiritual picture is what distinguishes a soul-aware woman from the ladies who only do lunch or the women of the Junior League or those who live for the PTA or civic causes or women who devote themselves almost entirely to the care of their families or the building of careers. I am a woman tending and strengthening my spiritual self. That is the defining difference in my approach to this journey toward old age.

The goal of my aging is clear: the renewal of my soul as my body deteriorates. That will be the focus of the following chapters. Some chapters will weed out what harms the soul. Others will carefully build on what strengthens and sweetens. I have set out the spiritual quest in the pages ahead. It is a redemptive and expansive dream.

How about you? Have I been able to articulate a yearning of yours? Do you want more than you're offered in the glossy pages of your favorite magazines? Does your soul jump at the possibility of life becoming better through the calendar year? If such a spiritual quest for joy sounds like an appealing goal in your life journey, then join me. You and I may have begun to lose our taste for lemonade. We may be exposing our souls to the possibilities of a quality of life that is better than we ever dreamed of at twenty or thirty or forty. We may be acquiring a taste for something with eternal significance—a taste for living water from the springs of the deep joy of the Lord.

Four

Faux Soul

faux *(fo)* adj. *Artificial; fake: faux pearls*

$\mathcal{M}$aking the right choices about the kind of spirituality you will pursue requires real perception these days. Let me explain.

Imagine this. You are at the movies. The show is incredible! It is undoubtedly going to sweep the Oscars! You are inspired and awe-filled. Laughter rings; tears flow. When it is over, no one breaks the spell by heading for the exits. The theater is hushed, transformed into a church-quiet holy place. The acting! The symbolism! The themes! The cinematography! Breathtaking! Impressive! Moving!

No one leaves the theater until the last credit fades from the screen. Slowly the crowd stands. They put on their coats. You start to overhear snatches of whispered conversation. You are curious. Did they like the parts you liked? Were they as moved as you were? But what's this? Hello? No one mentions the story line or the actors or the emotional wallop. Instead, everyone is talking about the credits. "The spelling was marvelous, and perfectly done, don't you think? And the rolling of the credit lines was incredibly paced. Such readability!"

What would you think? You might think that the theater had held a special showing for people with perceptual problems;

somehow you had mistakenly come at the wrong time. Wouldn't you wonder how everyone had managed to miss the main event, the movie itself?

Spirituality as Today's Trend

Our culture reminds me of that scenario. Today, spirituality is in. It is as if we are all in the same movie theater—looking for deeper life, hoping to be moved and inspired. Our usual American raucousness is being subdued with a contemplative quietness. From Oprah to Bill Clinton, almost everyone seems to be championing issues of the soul. Meditation is mainstream. Personal spiritual advisors are common. Fascination with angels and after-death experiences abounds. Studies indicate that most Americans not only believe in prayer but actually pray. In recent years even the *New York Times* best-seller book list has read like Sunday school material.

This trend toward spirituality is an amazing contrast to the stark secularization of recent decades. In some ways it really is an amazing turn, especially for those of us who remember the sixties when God was pronounced dead. But let's take a closer look at what's being discussed as our culture "leaves the theater" and debriefs inner life.

A Best-Seller's Definition of Soul Work

This definition of soul work recently captured America's attention and became the basis for a number-one best-seller:

> The aim of soul work . . . is a richly elaborated life, connected to society and nature, woven into the culture of family, nation and globe. The idea is not to be superficially adjusted, but to be profoundly connected in the

heart to ancestors and to living brothers and sisters in all
the many communities that claim our hearts.

In another place the author writes, "Soul is its own purpose
and end."[1]

Here is a definition of spirituality that embraces redemptive values: a deepening of life and a celebration of relationship
and connected, aware living. I like the sound of those values.
But this approach to inner life also makes me feel as if I just
walked out of the theater and something major is missing in the
discussion. Where, after all, is God in all this holy, connected,
deepened, interior living? At best in today's culture, even in its
most soulful moments, God is a sidebar. And Jesus is quickly
becoming a victim of political correctness, although new spiritual gurus are quick to repackage and market his principles as
their own.

Can you have spirituality without God? Our culture has a
deep resistance to facing any ultimate truth, including "God is."
Why doesn't our culture "get" God? The screen of human history
and experience points to God's holy interest and involvement in
human life. It is an awe-inspiring, breathtaking, mysteriously won-
drous story. In our own century, God's activity has been apparent
from the beaches of Normandy, where an evil empire began to fall,
to the toppling of the Berlin wall. Miracles of global, national, and
personal dimensions fill the screen. God's activity is in front of us
in living, breathing Technicolor! But as our culture debriefs the
meaning of what we witness before our eyes, notice how seldom
anyone talks about God as the focus of today's spirituality. Instead,
we get excited about the benefits of spirituality—"a richly elabo-
rated life" ("The spelling was marvelous"). We extol a life that is
profoundly "connected to society and nature" ("The rolling of the
credits had just the right amount of action"), and "to all the many

communities that claim our hearts" ("Such readability. I've never been so moved"). We are perceptually challenged spiritually. Even with our culture's fascination with soul, the main event is being overlooked. We are missing God.

Spirituality is in danger of becoming defined by a secular culture, a culture with problems in how it perceives most spiritual areas. Ignoring God in the process of developing spirituality, approaching inner life by focusing on the fringe issues and benefits, creates a kind of secular spirituality, an oxymoron if there ever was one.

Besides, it won't work. Trying to nurture inner life without God is like trying to birth a soul that is stuck in the birth canal. It's headed in the right direction—away from materialism, shallowness, and plasticity toward depth, quality, and interiority, but despite all its birth pains, it will never produce a living, breathing, healthy soul. Without a real spiritual birth that turns us toward God in humbleness and remorse and aligns us with his values, secular spirituality can at best produce a more refined, sophisticated version of the human toxic dump site. Look closely. The ultimate theme and focus of secular spirituality is *self*. A better self, a more inner-focused self, a more connected self, even a global community of selves, but self just the same. Self is the god of secular spirituality. If God is mentioned, he is usually defined by function—higher power, for example—not relationship. He is definitely not intimately embraced.

It is the endemic spirit of our age: that we define spirituality in terms of "me," not in terms of God.

I've noticed the home shopping channel uses the French word *faux* a lot. I imagine they think it has a classier sound than admitting that something is fake. Fake or not, the sellers are confident that even phony diamonds, emeralds, pearls, and leathers will look appealing under studio lights. They glitter. They shine. They sell! So it is with spirituality today. It glitters. It shines. It sells. But without God at its definitive core, whether or not the buyers and sellers realize it, it is faux just the same. Be careful when you're shopping around the Spiritual Shopping Network these days. All that appeals spiritually may not be true!

Friendship with God: The Goal of the Soul

The definition of soul work I embrace is classic. Its goal is the same goal as those who have sought God through the centuries. "The final goal is to become friends with God: We regard falling from God's friendship as the only thing dreadful and we consider becoming God's friend as the only thing worthy of honor and desire."[2]

Friendship with God, connectedness to God, is the goal of classic soul work. Soul is not its own purpose and end. The quality of our friendship with God determines the quality of our aging, our becoming. More connected relationships, a profound inner life, deeper contentment, and a richer existence are the qualities of life, the secondary benefits that flow out of knowing God.

In *Prayer: Finding the Heart's True Home*, Richard Foster explains how we can become perceptive about spirituality that is false and that which is true.

> As we live this way (abiding in Christ), we develop what Thomas à Kempis calls "a familiar friendship with Jesus." We become accustomed to his face. We distinguish the voice of the true Shepherd from that of religious hucksters in the same way professional jewelers distinguish a diamond from glass imitations—by acquaintanceship. When we have been around the genuine article long enough, the cheap and the shoddy become obvious.[3]

The obvious question to ask at this point is, What makes for a "familiar friendship"? Some of the same principles that make for quality human friendships can teach us about relating to God as his friend.

Recently Steve and I attended a small group meeting at the home of friends. It had been a stressful, hyperactive week in our lives. We had worked up until the very last minute, and with our minds still wrapped around other issues we arrived at their home, rang the front doorbell, and let ourselves in, as is our group's custom. We didn't realize how distracted we were until one of our friends asked, "Where are you two? It's like your bodies are here, but your minds are somewhere else." Her observation was right on. We were not fully engaged yet in the evening or in our friends' conversations. Our bodies were present, but we were somewhere else!

Sometimes I come to God in the same way. I am distracted, offering only my presence and little else. Though I long for deep connectedness, I thwart my own desires by trying to give him just my mind (what I think as opposed to what I feel). But God wants all of me. I can be vulnerable with God. There is great comfort in such intimacy. One of my friends who has suffered a great deal in life calls God "the God of Extreme Understanding." I like that name for God. That is the God I have met when I come naked-souled to him. The God of Extreme Understanding. We cannot be too honest or too open or too hurting or too sad to turn God away from embracing our souls. When I allow God to know my all of me, to connect at every personal level, body, mind, and soul, I develop a familiar friendship.

An additional characteristic of a familiar friendship with God became clear to me through another relational incident.

Many years ago I spent a lot of time with a woman who was struggling with several difficult problems at the time. During one of our conversations she asked me, "Valerie, am I just a ministry to you, or am I your friend?" I understood that no one wants to be considered someone else's project, and so I assured her of my fondness and friendship for her.

That was many years ago, but her question stuck with me. Recently, after many years of absence from each other, our paths crossed again. Eagerly I sat down with her over a cup of coffee to become reacquainted. She talked for two hours about her problems while I listened. She didn't ask me any questions. Our time together was one-sided, one-directional. Afterward I felt sad. I had wanted to be connected to her on more levels than just the problem areas of her life. I had wanted her to be a true friend, but she didn't seem to know how to be anything but a ministry. Our two hours together left me feeling more lonely than ever.

Sometimes I am like that with God. I come to him, dumping my dreads and problems in one-sided conversation. I am a ministry. Period. God is still the God of Extreme Understanding, even with that approach. But if I would also be a friend, I must learn to hear, feel, and perceive God's side. I confess that I often come and go from God's presence without touching him. He probably feels as lonely as he did before I came. I've been wondering, does my soul know how to embrace God, minister to him, bless and comfort him? Do I know how to delight him and "make his day," so to speak? Do I have compassion for his pain? Do I hurt where he hurts, smile where he smiles, love where he loves? Am I making our relationship, from his perspective, just another human project? Or am I on my way to being one of God's intimate friends?

Prayer: The Restorer of Well-Being

At my fortieth birthday my quality of life was at an all-time low. Cancer and the early deaths of my parents had shattered the kind of sense of well-being that we can sometimes have in life when everything seems to be going well. I needed more than circumstantial well-being to keep going in life. My sleepless nights and anxious days marked by extreme sadness probably could have been masked with medication. I would have felt better, at least, but I might not have done the interior soul work needed to address my real inner needs.

As I began prayerwalking, I discovered a sense of well-being based on God's love for me. Just as the psalmist declares, "This one thing I *know: God is for me!* I am trusting God—oh, praise his promises! I am not afraid of anything mere man can do to me" (Psalm 56:9–11 TLB). I began, through prayer, to understand that cancer could not take my life outside of God's will. All my fears of death, of life, of loss mattered much less in the light of God's love. *What can mere cancer do to me when God is on my side?* My soul pluckishly began to answer back to my fears.

A deep sense of connection to God was key to restoring my emotional health and inner strength. I was beginning to enjoy my life again. My anxiety was being healed by a sense of well-being with God. The healing I found through prayer opened my interest to other avenues of prayer. Shortly after my cancer, I discovered a twelve-step prayer system developed by Dick Eastman.[4] Just as I had moved beyond "Please heal me, God" in my emotional life, now I wanted to move beyond that point in my prayer life. Wonderful! The idea is that if you pray five minutes on each step, you will be able to spend an hour in prayer. I have found that whether I pray through the steps in an abbreviated way or devote an entire hour, I always feel more deeply connected to God. I have included some of the sources I use as jumping-off points for my own words and prayers. Using ancient hymns and prayers of Christians from all centuries and many countries deepens my sense of connection to these communities of the soul that share a common faith. The steps are as follows:

1. *Praise* (praising God for who he is)

O for a Thousand Tongues to Sing

O for a thousand tongues to sing
My great Redeemer's praise,
The glories of my God and King,
The triumphs of His grace.
Jesus! the name that charms our fears,
That bids our sorrows cease,
'Tis music in the sinner's ears,
'Tis life and health and peace.
Hear Him, ye deaf; His praise, ye dumb,
Your loosened tongues employ;
Ye blind, behold your Savior come;
And leap, ye lame, for joy.

Charles Wesley

I particularly relate to that last verse and identify with the deaf, dumb, and blind. We are all losers in the health lottery, but Christian joy is still our portion.

This hymn praises God for being our King and our Redeemer. While I pray this first section, my praise may focus on those attributes. At other times I may focus on one of the many names of God from Scripture, and my praise will exalt the characteristics of one particular name. Any praise song can be used in this manner to focus on a particular characteristic of God that is worthy of our praise. The possibilities are endless.

2. *Waiting* (taking the time to let God love you)

I Heard the Voice of Jesus Say

I heard the voice of Jesus say,
"Come unto me and rest,
Lay down, thou weary one, lay down
thy head upon my breast."
I came to Jesus as I was
Weary and weak and sad;
I found in Him a resting place,
And He has made me glad.

Horatius Bonar

I love the imagery of laying down my weary head on the breast of Jesus. Keeping that image in mind I still myself and let God love me. Again, any prayer or song that focuses on God's love can be used to help us receive God's love.

3. *Confession* (coming clean with God)

Out of My Bondage, Sorrow and Night

Out of my bondage, sorrow and night,
Jesus I come, Jesus I come;
Into thy freedom, gladness and light,
Jesus, I come to Thee.
Out of my sickness, into Thy health,
Out of my want and into Thy wealth,
Out of my sin and into Thyself,
Jesus, I come to Thee.

William T. Sleeper

My resistance to being open with God is sometimes due to my own sin. If my soul is harboring something nasty, coming to Jesus and laying my soul on his breast will comfort me for a while, but soon the intimacy with Jesus intensifies my sense of uncleanness. A clear picture of my soul's health is a natural outgrowth of closeness to God. Sometimes God nudges me toward inner health by bringing another person's name to mind or a kind of instant replay of something insensitive I said to someone. "Call her, Valerie. Make sure you have not sinned against her." Confession means I agree with God about my soul's health or lack of it. Confession restores my health and sense of connectedness to God.

4. *The Word* (reading God's Word)

This is the time to let God speak through the Bible. I use a one-year Bible format, reading the passage that corresponds with the date. I read it prayerfully, devotionally, marking any spots that seem to pertain to me or seem alive through a new understanding. I pray back to God anything he reveals to me in his Word.

For instance, on May 9 the assigned passage was Psalm 106:13–31. The fifteenth verse stood out: "So he gave them their demands, but sent them leanness in their souls" (TLB). I wondered what that interesting phrase, "leanness in their souls," meant. Then I realized that the characteristics of leanness of soul were in the verses that followed:

(v. 16) They were envious.
(vv. 19–20) They preferred things to the glorious presence of God himself.
(v. 24) They wouldn't believe God's solemn oath to care for them.
(v. 25) They pouted and mourned.

As I prayed over those verses, I saw my soul potentially in that condition, emaciated, starving, shriveled in on itself. I asked God to guard my soul from wanting anything more than I wanted his presence. I prayed that my life would not be characterized by pouting and doubting, but by trusting God.

5. *Intercession* (praying for a lost and dying world)

I am fond of the imagery of this prayer by Pierre Teilhard de Chardin, S. J., from the Oxford Book of Prayer:

> Since once again, Lord, . . . I have neither bread nor wine nor altar here on the Asian steppes, I lift myself far above symbols, to the pure majesty of the Real; and I, your priest, offer to you on the altar of the entire earth, the travail and suffering of the world. Yonder breaks the sun, to light the uttermost east, and then to its sheets of fire over the living surface of the earth, which wakens, shudders and resumes its appalling struggle.[5]

To pray about the "appalling struggle" of the entire world means to pray globally for a while. I pray for the outpouring of God's Spirit. I pray for a worldwide renewal. I pray for people in countries where there is war or famine or disease. I lift up believers around the world for the protection and blessing of God.

I also pray for those whose "appalling struggle" I know more personally. I pray for the requests made during our Bible study group. I pray for people I've seen on TV who are victims. I pray through a list of those who I know are hurting.

6. *Petition* (personal needs)

This is the prayer section in which we allow ourselves to be a ministry for a moment. The Psalms are full of prayers about personal needs. These can be prayed back to God.

> As the deer pants for streams of water,
>   so my soul pants for you, O God.

> My soul thirsts for God, for the living God.
>> When can I go and meet with God?
> My tears have been my food
>> day and night,
> while men say to me all day long,
>> "Where is your God?" . . . .
> Why are you downcast, O my soul?
>> Why so disturbed within me?
>> Put your hope in God,
>> for I will yet praise him,
>> my Savior and my God.

Psalm 42:1–3, 5

7. *The Word* (praying back God's words)

It is easy to pray in sync with God when we pray back his words from Scripture. The Psalms fit this format perfectly.

> Praise the LORD! Yes, really praise him! I will praise him as long as I live, yes, even with my dying breath.

> Don't look to men for help; their greatest leaders fail; . . . But happy is the man who has the God of Jacob as his helper, whose hope is in the Lord his God.

Psalm 146:1–5 TLB

8. *Thanksgiving* (what he has done)

When we praise God, we praise him for who he is. When we pray prayers of thanksgiving, we specifically focus on what he has done.

> Nothing has been capable, dear Lord, to hinder you from being all mine, neither heaven, nor your divinity, nor the gibbet of the cross: grant me the grace, that nothing may hinder me from being all yours. . . . Let the touch of yours,

which consecrates all things, sanctify my heart that it may be grateful to you.[6]

9. *Singing* (worship through melody)

Sing to God whatever song comes to you. Make it up. It doesn't need to rhyme. It just needs to flow from your heart. Enjoy!

10. *Meditation* (waiting in God's presence to love him)

I think of this as a quiet time to return God's hug. No words are necessary, just a quieted and loving heart pointed toward God.

11. *Listening* (taking the time to hear God)

Prayer is not just God listening while we talk. It is also receiving from him. Don't monopolize your prayer time with a one-sided conversation. Give God a chance to respond. Practice stillness and wait for a nudge from God.

12. *Praise* (for who God is)

I like to end by singing something upbeat and joyful or quoting a praise psalm.

If you are interested in prayerwalking that somewhat follows the above format, I've created a prayerwalking tool, a cassette tape, set to an aerobic music pace, with a guided prayer format. For other details, check the back of this book.

Classic Soul

Aging has given me an appreciation for things that are not trendy but classic. Classic-cut jeans and suits appeal. I love the patina of my wood antiques; they just get better with age. I collect American pottery because I know it is timeless—as beautiful one hundred years from now as it was the day it was created.

When it comes to my soul, I am experiencing the same directional desire. I want classic, tried-and-true intimacy with

God. I do not want just human connectedness, however global. I want to experience my Soul Mate. I do not want to settle for being in tune with nature and ancestors. Yes, I am interested in depth and tired of superficiality. But I realize any version of deeper life, apart from God, will not satisfy. My soul was created to be a God-fit. I am incomplete without him, frustrated and dissatisfied with other substitutes. God is the goal of soul; all other hungers are symptomatic of the soul's longing to connect to its soul mate—God.

Who is this God? He is Creator God. The Ancient of Days is my God. Picture him fomenting creation from a bouillabaisse of ex nihilo words. Universes of microorganisms and galaxies of planets and stars swirl into existence at his command, while the intricacies of genetics, DNA patterns, and chemical marinades—endorphins, seratonin, dopamine—subtly make possible the continuance of life. He speaks the word and feathered and finned things morph animated from his lips and tongue. Lightning flashes, molecules swirl, the noise of creation thunders, and when he speaks his very thoughts appear.

Finally God creates a wonder, the jewel of creation, the apex of his genius. He gives it eternality and individuality, with a strong capacity for both corruption and holiness. God particularly loves this creation, endowing it with his own image. Satan fights and schemes to destroy this soul so close to God's heart. This wonder of creation is the human soul. Soul was uniquely created and fitted for intimacy with God.

This God who holds my soul so dear is Creator God. He is the same who formed Eve from the rib of a delighted Adam, the same who thought woman was an excellent idea. He is woman-friendly.

I want my spirit to be deeply connected with laughing, wrinkled Sarah's God—the one who did not despise her age but surprised her with her heart's deepest desire: a pregnancy, a son, a blessing. I want this same God to form my laughter, my old-age surprises, my blessings.

My God is Queen Esther's God. He is a God who thought it appropriate to partner with a beautiful woman, who "brought her to the kingdom for such a time as this" to defeat evil and preserve a nation. I want to be a kingdom player, brought to the kingdoms of my influence for such a time as this. I want to be a part of his grand design. I want to play on his team.

I want the kind of devoted, expressive intimacy that Mary knew when she perfumed Jesus' feet and dried them with her hair. When she was criticized for such a seemingly inappropriate act, Jesus himself was her defender. Jesus knows the feminine heart and is comfortable with the devotion of women. Our femininity is appropriate to him. This Jesus is my God.

The Jesus who hung naked and crucified is mine as well. I recognize in that agonizing scene the picture of the seriousness of my sin—the consequences of the corruption of my soul. I agree with his Father that my condition of soul can never be good enough for salvation without Jesus' part. I need a Savior; I accept the gift of a Savior. My soul is liberated from self and Satan by God himself. This Jesus is my Savior, God's own Son.

My classic and tried God is the same who comforted women through the ages whether they cried from lonely prison dungeons or over the ravage of war, the death of children, the loss of husbands, the horror of rape, or any other feminine heartbreak. When I die I want my soul to experience the comfort of the arms of this God who knows and loves the feminine soul.

Simply put, I want God.

I want my soul to be developing toward God with a spirituality that is genuine and authentic, not trendy. I do not want to sit in the cultural theater, read the best-sellers, and listen to group discussions and still manage to miss the main event: God.

If I Have Not Love, I Am Nothing

Faux spirituality is nothing new. As I listen to the attractive verbiage about soul today, I hear the ancient biblical warning of 1 Corinthians 13. When I see how those with spiritual-word giftedness are able to motivate our culture toward a kind of deeper life and realize the fortunes being made by spiritual gurus who can talk inspirationally, I hear the echo of the tongues of men and angels. Bring out the gongs! Strike the cymbals! The spouting of beautiful-sounding spiritual words is an old card game. And for just the price of a video or an expensive but fascinating seminar, you can be taken in too.

I watched a talk show that caught my attention. I was fascinated. The participants were actually praying. The words had a holy ring to them. But later I learned that this teacher of prayer who had wowed and inspired me had been married many times (and he looked to be only middle-aged). I am amazed at the willingness of our culture to overlook such misalignment of private and public living. We should be wary of people who presume to teach spirituality but whose private lives indicate enormous gaps between their words and reality. We should be offended at such public posturing and presumption by those whose private lives are disastrous. It may be nothing but religious noise. Offensive religious noise. The cup is polished, but there is no love inside. It is shiny and cheap and tinny and false. Faux soul.

The Litmus Test of Friendship with God

What then? How can we age toward genuine spirituality? How do I know if I am a friend of God's? Scripture says that without love I am nothing (1 Corinthians 13:2). All my spirituality is measured by how full my cup is with God and his love. This is soulfulness. This is spirituality.

Love is the soul's most excellent spiritual journey. Love guards against the negative tendencies of a soul gathering years. It is the antidote for all ugliness that can easily accumulate through the years. It tempers anger. It tames superiority. It sweetens sadness. It opens the door of connectedness to surprising communities of the heart striking a blow at old-age loneliness. It fills in the gaps of the soul, replacing cup polishing and image-making with authentic alignment of the inner and outer persons. Love guards against the tendency to care less and less what others think or feel, the wounding of others when we lay it all on the table. It checks the untended soul's characteristics of offensiveness, orneriness, pettiness, and smallness. Love keeps us from doing things only for show. Love redeems the corruption of our aging.

And although love has been overused and so weakly defined that it is in danger of becoming an anemic bore at its mere mention, real love, not its cheap imitations, is still the true test of spirituality.

And so, spiritual travelers, aging journeyers, soul sisters, those born spiritually and those in the spiritual birth canal looking for something deeper: It is time. It is time to silence the resounding gongs and cymbals, the religious noise.

It is time to be God's friend, a woman who reflects his values, his spirituality, his heart. Classic soul is our goal. Love enters and takes center stage. Here then is "the most excellent way" revealed by God, who, you will find, well knows the feminine soul.

Five

Color Me Patient,
Color Me Kind

*God loves us; not because we are loveable but
because He is love, not because He needs to receive
but because He delights to give.*

—C. S. Lewis, *Letters of* C. S. *Lewis*

Love is patient, love is kind.

—1 Corinthians 13:4

*W*hat's your puppy's name?" the stranger asked. *Could he be
talking about Olivia?* I looked down at my fourteen-year-old
"puppy." Her head was tilted to the side in the manner so characteristic of West Highland white terriers. It was body language
for, "What did he say? What did he call me?" She knows she's
adorable when she does that. But adorable or not, believe me,
it has been a long time since anyone had called her "puppy."

She was a terror in her salad days—a real jock. Through
the years our veterinarian has frequently practiced sports medicine on Olivia, mending the injuries she sustained while playing soccer with our sons and their friends. One broken toe. One

hip surgery. Countless times of having her breath knocked out of her by the "direct hit" of a soccer ball. She was constantly being run over and stepped on.

All our efforts to protect her failed. She barked her head off when we tied her up. We tried to keep her inside, but she would not be "benched." She knew how angry her peeing in the house made us. It was her trump card. She played it regardless of personal consequences. Anything to be one of the guys! We learned it was better to let her play than to have to clean up pee. Olivia's theory of people training was that there were no bad people. We all proved trainable to her will.

Just a few years ago she was one of the kids. Dog years have made her old. I have spent the past months carrying her up and down the staircases of our home. She brazenly sleeps on our couches, a no-no in her younger years. She seems to think she's paid her dues and now has earned the right to set her own rules. She throws up a lot. You can smell her a room away. She has other old-age behavior problems. Some people have tried to gently suggest we should consider putting her to sleep, but my heart says it's not time. I'm attached to this furry rapscallion who has lived with so much heart through the years. Besides, I hope to model for my sons how "old things" should be treated.

"My 'puppy's' name is Olivia," I answered the stranger. I didn't correct him about her age. But what was this? Maybe it was hearing the word "puppy" again. Maybe being called a puppy is to an old dog what getting carded is to a middle-aged woman. I don't know. But this same dog, who whines at the bottom of the stairs to be carried up, was now running through the yard, waggy-tailed and perky. She was outright flirting with this man, barking her "Come play" bark.

Olivia, you are totally shameless!

Little Kindnesses Can Go a Long Way

Little kindnesses can go a long way.

Olivia, I completely understand, I thought. *We old girls need our perks from time to time!* I laughed, remembering that just the weekend before I had also benefited from a mistaken label given me by a stranger. It was nothing really, but it struck me in a long-forgotten place of my soul.

I was in the Charlotte airport moving through a cafeteria line. We were iced in and no planes were leaving. No one was happy, including me. Airline employees had grown impatient with the demands of travelers trying to find alternate plans. My own plans to get home that night—in time to see my son in the lead of the high school musical—were fading. I was so looking forward to it, and now it looked as though I was going to miss this big night in Justin's life.

Rats! The South! They don't seem to be able to deal with the slightest weather here! I thought.

I juggled my cart, briefcase, and coat in one arm and slid a tray along the cafeteria line, eventually placing an unappealing piece of pizza on my tray. When I came to the cashier, I had to shift everything again trying to find my wallet, which was buried deep in the bottom of my briefcase. Without even looking up, I apologized for causing a delay.

"That's okay, baby," a woman's southern voice gently answered. It belonged to the cashier, a black woman at least twenty years younger than I. Baby? The term of endearment in such an unlikely place surprised me. No one has called me "baby" for years. I am in the stage of life where people tend to think of me more as their mother, not their baby. How unusual that this young woman reached across the gap of years, race, and culture to grace me with the word "baby." It may have been simply a cultural practice for her, but it had worked some magic deep inside of me. One word had calmed my troubled world and what had been a frustrating day now seemed full of softer, gentler, and sweeter possibilities.

"That's okay, baby!" I love the South!

I know some people think such terms of endearment are meaningless, demeaning even. But I like that it doesn't matter who you are—rascal or saint, rich woman or poor woman, young or old, black or white or any shade in between—you can just walk through a cafeteria line and for a few seconds be somebody's baby, or honey, or darlin'.

Small Graces, Soul Graces

I guess we all love to be on the receiving end of someone else's affection, even if it's only in passing. Better yet to be on the receiving end of affection from the people who actually know us. Wouldn't it be wonderful to end up in our older years like that Grandma in the Hallmark commercials? It's her birthday, and I'd say she's getting up there in the one-hundred-year-old zone, where Willard Scott will put her picture on the *Today Show* and call her a "beautiful girl." She's surrounded by people who love her. Even when she barks, "I want my card!" they overlook her eccentricity and laugh as if such old-age childishness is adorable and charming. I hope when I'm wrinkled to the consistency of corduroy and my cake is roaring with one hundred candles, that some Willard Scott wanna-be will call me a "beautiful girl" and my children and grandchildren will think me adorable, even if my behavior isn't.

Small graces make the world go 'round. We receive these blessings from both strangers and friends: a neighbor who occasionally cleans the whole block of sidewalks with his snowblower; friends who come to our children's school performances and rave about how good they are (even if they aren't!); someone who breaks the tie in a store line by smiling and motioning for you to go first; the guy on the block who always buys the fund-raising candy, or sausage and cheese, or magazines from the middle school kids; the teacher who has an encouraging word for every parent; the note senders; the phone callers; people who cheerfully deal with the public on their jobs; police officers who give us warnings instead of tickets; people who give compliments; a stranger who says "puppy" instead of old dog, or "baby" instead of "ma'am."

What would this world be like without such kindnesses? Small kindnesses are more than they appear to be. Small kindnesses are small loves, small pieces of someone's caring. They may be done or said in passing; they may be nothing more than cultural politeness; they may not even be intentional, but sometimes, though small, they are enough.

But as delightful as these small kindnesses may be, how much better to receive the gift of another person's soul. Sometimes only a deeper giving, a coming together at a soul meeting place—a shared confidence, a deep compassion expressed, an extravagant gesture of caring, can touch us where we need to be touched: soul to soul. We need to be able to give and receive "soul graces" as well as small graces.

> The capacity to give to others out of the depth's of one's soul is a rich delight. Being a good neighbor who is willing to lend a hand to someone in need is pleasant enough. How much more delight is there (at least there should be) in offering one's soul—one's core possession that will last for eternity—to another for his supreme good? This joy is beyond words.[1]

"Love is patient, love is kind," are some of the most beautiful words I know. They speak of the giving dimension of love, a lifestyle of graciousness, both of small graces and of the deeper offerings of the soul. "Love is patient, love is kind," runs the gamut of the kindness scale, from a simple, yet appropriate word in passing, when peevishness might have been in order, to the sharing of life on the most intimate connected levels, day after day and year after year. It suggests a consistent, predictable offering of grace, a lifestyle of kind gestures and words, whether given to another for only a second or for a lifetime in the extended day-by-day togetherness of life. How bleak this world would be without those who practice small kindnesses, small loves. Worse yet—how desperate this world would be without those who know how to give from their souls, who walk through dark places with others, who comfort, who cheer, who connect, who hang in there no matter what.

In third grade we thought love was having your valentine's box stuffed with valentines. In high school we thought love was having a date for the prom. As adult women we thought love was having a social calendar crowded with invitations. We were wrong.

Real love is not just being the one-way object of another's affections but a kind of connecting that brings us together, soul to soul. Giving is always involved in that kind of love. Only real love can redeem the most tangled human dilemmas.

"I Think My Life Must Be Happier Than the Lives of 95 Percent of the People on Planet Earth"

Robertson McQuilkin is such a lover. He has written about his life with his wife, Muriel, who suffers from Alzheimer's. Several years ago he stepped down as president of Columbia Bible

College and Seminary (now Columbia International University) to care for her. His own eloquent words describe the mysteries of the love he has discovered as he's given her his soul.

> Seventeen summers ago, Muriel and I began our journey into the twilight. It's midnight now, at least for her, and sometimes I wonder when dawn will break. Even the dread Alzheimer's disease isn't supposed to attack so early and torment so long. Yet, in her silent world, Muriel is so content, so lovable. If Jesus took her home, how I would miss her gentle, sweet presence. Yes, there are times when I get irritated, but not often. It doesn't make much sense to get angry. And besides, perhaps the Lord has been answering the prayer of my youth to mellow my spirit.
>
> Once, though, I completely lost it. In the days when Muriel could still stand and walk and we had not resorted to diapers, sometimes there were "accidents." I was on my knees beside her, trying to clean up the mess as she stood, confused, by the toilet. It would have been easier if she weren't so insistent on helping. I got more and more frustrated. Suddenly, to make her stand still, I slapped her calf—as if that would do any good. It wasn't a hard slap, but she was startled. I was, too. Never in our 44 years of marriage had I ever so much as touched her in anger or in rebuke of any kind. Never; wasn't even tempted, in fact. But now, when she needed me most . . .
>
> Sobbing, I pled with her to forgive me—no matter that she didn't understand words any better than she could speak them. So I turned to the Lord to tell him how sorry I was. It took me days to get over it. Maybe God bottled those tears to quench the fires that might ignite again some day. . . .

Recently, a student wife asked me . . . "Don't you ever get tired?"

"Tired? Every night. That's why I go to bed."

"No, I mean tired of . . ." and she tilted her head toward Muriel, who sat silently in her wheelchair, her vacant eyes saying, "No one at home just now." I responded to Cindi's question, "Why, no, I don't get tired. I love to care for her. She's my precious. . . ."

Love is said to evaporate if the relationship is not mutual, if it's not physical, if the other person doesn't communicate, or if one party doesn't carry his or her share of the load. When I hear the litany of essentials for a happy marriage, I count off what my beloved can no longer contribute, and I contemplate how truly mysterious love is . . .

What some people find so hard to understand is that loving Muriel isn't hard. They wonder about my former loves—like my work. . . . "Do you miss being president?" [a student] asked as we sat in our little garden. I told him I'd never thought about it, but, on reflection, no. As exhilarating as my work had been, I enjoyed learning to cook and keep house. No, I'd never looked back.

But that night I did reflect on his question and turned to the Lord. "Father, I like this assignment, and I have no regrets. But if a coach puts a man on the bench, he must not want him in the game. You needn't tell me, of course, but I'd like to know—why didn't you keep me in the game?"

I didn't sleep well that night and awoke contemplating the puzzle. Muriel was still mobile at that time, so we set out on our morning walk around the block. She wasn't too sure on her feet, so we went slowly and held hands as we always do. This day I heard footsteps behind me and looked back to see the familiar form of a local derelict behind us. He staggered past us, then turned and looked us up and down. "Tha's good. I likes 'at," he said. "Tha's real good. I likes it." He turned and headed back down the street, mumbling to himself over and over, "Tha's good. I likes it."

When Muriel and I reached our little garden and sat down, his words came back to me. Then the realization hit me; the Lord had spoken through an inebriated old derelict. "It is *you* who are whispering to my spirit, 'I likes it, tha's good,'" I said aloud. "I may be on the bench, but if you like it and say it's good, that's all that counts..."

I think my life is happier than the lives of 95 percent of the people on planet Earth.[2]

Tears That Tell Stories

When I share this story with other women, sometimes it brings tears. Why does it touch us so? Perhaps we cry because the sweet sadness in this couple's tale of terrible loss is moving. Or maybe we women cry at this story because it captures our fear of aging and becoming helpless and dependent.

Some of the tears are probably tears of longing. Some of us have never been loved even close to the way Muriel is loved by Robertson. Most women yearn to have a Robertson in their lives, someone who cares and adores "for better or worse." Hearing Robertson describe his love for Muriel may make us realize that we are disconnected at our deepest levels. Robertson's love for Muriel spotlights the deep isolation of our souls. It appears that Robertsons are hard to come by in life.

Some of the tears are responses to the profound beauty of Robertson's love. He wonders why he has been benched. We sense one of the answers to his question is that his love is a high-water mark given to an observing world. Through his sacrifice, we have been given a measuring device for the quality of the love we give to those in our care. We cry not only because others have fallen short for us, we cry because we realize we have not proven to be anywhere near as loving to others as Robertson is to Muriel.

A Picture of God's Love

Robertson's love is more than a high-water mark, however. It is a picture of how God loves us. Like Robertson's love for Muriel, the love of God defies logic and reason. God's love challenges our stingy definitions of love. It is totally without condition.

It is a love for the utterly unworthy, a love that proceeds from God who is love. It is a love lavished on others without a thought of whether they are worthy or not. It proceeds from the nature of the lover, rather than from the merit of the beloved.[3]

God loves us because of who he is . . . it is his nature. His love is not measured out to us in carefully leveled teaspoons corresponding to our responsiveness or lack of response, our attractiveness or our repulsiveness—it is not doled out to us according to what we deserve. Instead, he lavishes—mounds, heaps, piles on—his love, like a sundae overdipped with sweet chocolate syrup running over the sides, over the tabletop, down the sides, and onto the floor.

Like Robertson, God loves though "the relationship is not mutual, we do not communicate, and we fail to carry our share of the load." God loves because of who he is.

Prodigal Daughter

My heart goes out to Robertson and Muriel. I also understand. I lost my father when I was twenty-six. After encephalitis burned out his brain he lived for the next four-and-a-half years without his mind. A different man lived in my father's body for the rest of his life. This man did not know us or love us. He did not even remember us. We never saw a glint of recognition in his eyes for any of us. He would smile for others sometimes, but rarely for us. He was nonverbal, apparently nonthinking, unable to learn or remember. He was pathetically confused, sometimes agitated. He shuffled when he walked. Getting him into a car was a struggle. You had to bend his body, duck his head. All the while he struggled against you, stiff, insecure, lacking the understanding of what you were trying to do for him. He needed constant care. Although he was only sixty-five when encephalitis struck him, my father spent those last sad years of his life in a nursing home.

The small grace of a stranger stands out during this time. One day my father managed to "escape." He walked out the front door of the nursing home, down a busy street, and let himself into the home of a stranger. A woman lived there alone. Imagine having someone in his condition walk into your home! She might have shot this intruder or at least called the police. But after her initial shock, she realized he must be from the nursing home. Amazingly, she did not immediately call them to come get him. Her heart went out to my father. She wondered if this man had eaten anything but institutional food lately. She sat him down in her own kitchen, set the table for him, and prepared a home-cooked breakfast. She carried on a one-way conversation. He apparently enjoyed it immensely. When he was through, she called the home and they came for him. Thank heavens love is sometimes patient and kind even to strangers who are disoriented and cannot speak, who walk into your kitchen bright and early some unsuspecting morning.

Unfortunately small graces escaped me then. I was too heartbroken to be comforted by them. This was an awkward time for me spiritually. I felt that God was somehow to blame for my father's illness. I was confused, angry. Every time I was with my dad my heart sank deeper into hopelessness. My faith weakened until, one day, I lifted my fist to God and declared that "I do not believe in you anymore. Either you are too impotent or too uncaring or too cruel to help my father. So, what good are you anyway?" I became the prodigal daughter. I left the Father, not even asking for my inheritance. I wanted nothing more to do with this God.

I was still a pastor's wife, but my heart was the heart of a rebel. It is extremely awkward to be a pastor's wife with a deficit in the faith department. I faked it a lot. I still went through the motions at church, but my heart was not in it. While the rest of the congregation sang "'Tis So Sweet to Trust in Jesus," my heart was mouthing, "Baloney, baloney, baloney."

My dad's illness was the beginning of anger's foothold in my life . . . a toehold of sin into my soul. Anger is what I bleed when I'm hurt. If I could just learn to cry when I'm hurt, I would be so much more lovable! It would take me years to unpeel the layers of anger that built up during this time in my life. But that process began with an encounter from someone who reached out to me with her own soul.

I did not fool God. He saw past the inappropriate expression of anger right into my broken heart. An older, more spiritual woman saw it too. She sensed my despair and estrangement and asked if she could pray with me. She gave me this image. "God has been waiting for you for a long time, Valerie. He is so delighted you have finally come. You are exhausted from your struggle. He wants to hold you like a Father. He wants to put his arms around you and never let you go." I let out an enormous soul-sigh and tears at her words.

She continued, "God is laughing with delight over you. His head is thrown back and his arms are around you. He is laughing, laughing, laughing with joy over you."

She didn't say these words, but my soul registered them: "That's okay, baby!"

Her words soothed my soul. For the first time I saw myself as the prodigal daughter, whipped by life and returning home to the arms of her Father. My soul had been rigid for so long that I felt an almost immediate softening and relaxing. This was more than a small grace. It was a gesture that broke through to my soul. She met me soul to soul and let me know that I could come back home. It was okay for the rebellious angry prodigal to come back to God. From my perspective, I thought I didn't deserve to be loved. I knew I was prickly and unlovable. But God's love has no conditions. It is not earnable or dissolvable. God broke through to me with this picture of his extreme understanding. He loved my heartbroken child-self back to himself.

Although I had grown up in the church, I never realized God's love for me until I was prodigal and undeserving. My self-exile was the vehicle through which I personally began to understand the unconditional love of God. Up until then, God's love was abstract, only a lovely theory, a beautiful Bible verse, a catchy phrase from Sunday school days.

It was a rare turning point in my life.

The Freedom of Unconditional Loving

God's love stands in such contrast to our human ways of loving. Have you ever noticed how so many of our human loves are more or less conditional? We practice conditional Christmas card sending, keeping lists of who sent Christmas cards last year, so we know whom to include this year. We keep track of who entertained us and to whom we need to reciprocate. We withdraw from relationships that wound us, even if unintentionally. We edit people out of our lives who are too needy or time-consuming. We practice boundaries and measure out love in tiny teaspoons based on merit or loveliness or return on investment.

No wonder we feel isolated and lonely. Yet, even though we admire a man like Robertson, most of us would not want to trade places with him. Many people would look at Robertson's life and think he is enslaved by Muriel's needs. But Robertson may be the most free man of all. He is free to love Muriel regardless of her "lack of responsiveness, or her inability to communicate or carry her share of the load." Robertson's love for Muriel transcends the human plane of love and reflects the unconditional love of God.

I recognize that there are certain benefits to life interpreted through the love of God. Loving with God's love frees us from practicing the human love that binds us, shrinks our spirits, and arrests the development of our souls. Understanding and practicing God's unconditional love is key to successful aging, to the care of our souls, to true spirituality. Practicing the unconditional love of God expands us. Our capacity to connect increases. Superficiality is challenged because we become more deeply involved and attached.

Loneliness is not a problem for those who love without editing, measuring, and calculating. We could do something wild like throwing the Christmas card list away and send seasons greetings because we care, not out of social obligation. That's freeing! We can keep entertaining people who do not or cannot return the favor, and not notice. We do not have to figure out whether this person is deserving or that person is a good guy or a bad guy. No more tit for tat.

Practicing the unconditional love of God toward others even allows us to patiently hang in there with a difficult personality and return graciousness for rudeness. We are free to live on a higher plane.

Do I have my act together as a giver of unconditional love? Sometimes. And sometimes not. But more and more, I'm aware of operating with an acceptance that outdistances my own natural inclinations. I've noticed a growing sense of freedom in my relationships I didn't have when I was younger. It is a direction, a goal that I am building into my soul intentionally.

As I look back on my life, a more unconditional love for others, based on God's unconditional love for me (not on who I perceived them to be) would have simplified many of my relational dilemmas. I could have been more patient with Trevor the Terrible instead of being so quick to judge him. I would have been kind enough to be the one sending the cards to my friends, whether or not I heard from them (after all, too often my friends have had to hang in there with *my* nonresponsiveness). Relationships would have improved life if I had been freed from measuring out love to others based on what I thought they deserved.

When I was thirty-something, I remember the sense of panic I felt when I realized the inescapable demands of a neighborhood ministry to children into which I felt God was calling our family. There were no "office hours." We were sitting ducks available at any hour. In my forties I am softer, more flexible. I am much more aware of having received the patient, kind love of God, and that awareness has given me more willingness to hang in there than I had as a younger woman. At forty there is more kindness, more of a willingness to patiently share my soul, more flexibility in my schedule for someone in need. Yes, I blow it sometimes. But directionally, I am on the right path.

God's love simplifies all our relational dilemmas. The answer to the people who perplex us is love. God's love, expressed in us, makes us generous of heart. God's love in us transforms our character, enabling us to love a world of lovely and unlovely others. God's love, in us, makes us consistent in character, as kind to the unlovely as to those to whom we are naturally attracted. When we love this way, our souls develop beautifully, connected deeply to both God and to other people.

Love is the soul's greatest beautifier!

Am I a Lover?

But what if I don't *feel* loving? How can I love? Have you ever asked yourself that about someone who strolls into your life, covered with burrs and prickly points, who obviously wants a piece of you, but your first inclination is to turn and run the other way? C. S. Lewis shows the way through this briar patch of our feelings (or lack of them) toward other people.

> Love, in the Christian sense, does not mean an emotion.
> It is a state, not of the feelings, but of the will; that state
> of the will which we have naturally about ourselves, and
> must learn to have about other people.[4]

Time and again I have experienced a mysterious process happening in relationship to other people. Sometimes people enter my life and, initially, I am not drawn to them by anything even close to affection. But over time, an almost imperceptible change takes place. I hear their stories, vicariously experience their pain, and compassion begins to draw me. What was a "state of will" in my relating to them becomes a "state of care." I have moved beyond my own inclinations toward them.

This is one of the encouraging evidences that God is active in my life. I am watching God grow me into having more patience with the people and situations to which I am not naturally inclined. Initially, I have my own perceptions. But just as God saw past my rebellion to my hurt, I began to perceive more than what's on the surface.

I am learning how to say, "That's okay, baby!" in so many ways. I hear the aggravating whine of a child, but I also become aware of the need that drives the whine. "That's okay, baby! Let me help you with that."

My adolescent son may pelt me with complaints of "it's not fair," and I can forego throwing life back at him with an unsympathetic, "Well, life isn't fair. Grow up!" because I remember how it felt when I thought I was a persecuted adolescent. "That's okay, baby! I know it's frustrating, but you won't be a teenager forever! Someday you'll be in charge."

When a college kid drops in to talk about his love life just at my bedtime, I can remember that I, too, lived on Hong Kong time at that age—up all night, sleeping half of the day—and that at nineteen, a broken heart can't always wait for the comfort that comes in the morning. "That's okay, baby!" my I'm-old-enough-to-be-your-mother mouth consoles. "If I were your age, I'd grab you in a second!"

It's a mistake to wait for affectionate feelings before we show patient loving care for another person. Show caring, "position the will," and you may be surprised down the relational road how your feelings may align. Whether the feelings ever emerge, we can still be loving by an act of the will demonstrated in kindnesses toward that person.

The "Little Way"

Loving with patient kindness those we do not naturally love is a lifestyle endorsed by a Christian woman named Therese of Lisieux or the "Little Flower." She felt that God is especially pleased when we quietly serve others with small kindnesses. She understood that while these everyday gentlenesses may seem inconsequential, they actually serve a tremendous purpose in our souls. They break the backbone of our own self-preoccupation. They conquer the "me" inside.

An incident from her lifestyle of small kindnesses is particularly delightful. Therese lived in a community that included a woman she found particularly unlovable. Conceited, ignorant, full of herself, this woman was a daily irritation. But Therese didn't avoid the woman. She wrote, "I set myself to treat her as if I loved her best of all."[5]

Did Therese always feel loving? Her writings indicate she did not. But was she loving? Yes, she was. Therese was able to express love to an unlovely because of her own character. And she succeeded. After Therese's death, this woman said, "During her life, I made her really happy."[6] When we love in challenging situations, when we initiate kindnesses toward difficult people, we indicate that we are intimate friends of God; we are taking on his character. We are not just cup polishing, plastering on a smiling face while we feel hostile inside. We are aligning our outer expression to God's love while it forms our inner character.

Saints often understand and model this love for the rest of us in the puny-souled world. It is interesting but not too surprising that the world does not remember the name of the woman who received Therese's love. She is remembered simply as "the woman." She is an old story, a "taker." By contrast, the world has never forgotten Therese. Saint Therese she is sometimes called. Therese was a "giver" and the world remembers its saints.

The Many High-Water Marks of Love

Love has many personalities. Sometimes it is extroverted, arms opened wide, rosy-cheeked, hugging and kissing the world, squeezing every relational moment from the day. And sometimes love has an introverted, quiet, steady, sure style that listens, lends an appropriate book, and drops a note.

Whatever its style, love that is patient and kind sets the high-water mark for a watching world. The world can't help but notice its Robertsons and its Thereses. The world can't help but notice great lovers.

> The love for equals is a human thing—of friend for friend, brother for brother. It is to love what is loving and lovely. The world smiles.
>
> The love for the less fortunate is a beautiful thing—the love for those who suffer, for those who are poor, the sick, the failures, the unlovely. This is compassion and it touches the heart of the world.
>
> The love for the more fortunate is a rare thing—to love those who succeed where we fail, to rejoice without envy with those who rejoice, the love of the poor for the rich,

or the black man for the white man. The world is always bewildered by its saints.

And then there is the love for the enemy—love for one who does not love you but mocks, threatens, and inflicts pain. The tortured's love for the torturer. This is God's love. It conquers the world.[7]

Look in the mirror of your soul. What do you see? A taker or a giver? A great saintly lover or a woman whose loves are only of a human, conditional dimension? The path to a love that can even love an enemy is paved with small kindnesses practiced with friends, with those less fortunate, and with all the many random life connections in between. It's a life direction which, through practice, can form our soul to the dimensions of God's own heart.

Contrary to popular thought, great lovers are not born; they are formed in the consistent practice of patient kindnesses offered in a world of lovely and unlovely others. And contrary to popular thought, which holds that having your valentine's box stuffed with valentines makes you a real winner in life, understand that, in the end, it is only the patient, kind lovers who positively impact the world at all.

Yes, the world is always bewildered by its saints. But bewildered or not, the world is also blessed by its saints, those patient, kind healers who carry the love of God into all their human relationships.

"That's okay, baby!"

How the world needs that healing word from God. Say it as a blessing. Say it with hope that points a lost world to God's love. Say it to the prodigal. Pronounce it in dark places. Wrap it like a hug around some lonely heart. Band-Aid it over some soul wound. Find the ways to say "That's okay, baby!" and fill this aching world with the softer, gentler, and sweeter possibilities of God's love. Sing it! Whisper it! Shout it! Live it!

Stretch your soul to the dimensions of the saint's high-water mark and then listen. You will hear it, that inner voice of God's approval whispering to your soul, "Tha's good, I likes 'at." And if he likes it, that's what counts.

Six

❧

It's Not Easy Being Green

Mirror, mirror on the wall,
who is the fairest of them all?

—Snow White's (aging) stepmother

Love does not envy.

—1 Corinthians 13:4b

$\mathcal{T}$he other day I was chatting with a successful professional woman. She exudes a confident, comfortable-in-her-own-skin kind of air in her middle years. When I complimented her on it, she told me that it had not always been so. In high school particularly, she thought herself a social misfit. Even though she was a leader in student government and on the high honor roll, she never felt successful. That was because the place she measured her success, or lack of it, was at the roller rink.

When it came time for the boys to ask the girls to skate, she usually watched from the sidelines while some other girl skated with the boy she liked. "Back then, Valerie," she confided, "I would have traded my good grades and student leadership for one turn around the rink with the right guy."

Well, maybe who you are going to skate with at the roller rink this weekend is no longer of great importance, but who hasn't experienced watching someone else take that turn around the rink—the one you wished you could have? Who hasn't sat on the sidelines wishing for some other woman's advantage?

Even if your skates have been collecting dust in some forgotten closet corner for years, in your career you may have known that same feeling as you stood by and watched some young professional basking in the light of quick and easy success while you continued to plod on unnoticed and unapplauded.

Or maybe there is someone in your life who gets all the attention—the attention you would like to receive. It just seems she is always basking in the warm glow of others' notice while you are overshadowed.

Maybe some other woman's life seems so easy, while yours is so hard. If you asked yourself, "What would it take for me to be really happy?" and you were totally honest, would the answer be some other woman's life or some piece of another woman's life? If so, then I know exactly how you feel. Let me share an experience I had.

Someone Was Taking My Turn Around the Rink

I was attending a meeting of Christian broadcasters. Broadcasting was a new career field for me. I had spent the years right out of college teaching music during the week and singing on the weekends for churches, women's conferences, and weddings. It hit me immediately; this room was filled with men. I was one of a few women there. A young woman—quite talented—was singing. Initially I was enjoying her immensely, right along with all the other guys, so to speak.

Then something happened. I looked around the room. The audience was absorbed with her singing, as if they had become

a part of every lilt and twist. She held them with her voice like
putty in her hand. And then the thought struck me. She had
just turned this audience of grown professional Christian men
into a kind of collective Pillsbury Dough Boy!

Just as a high school girl measures her social success by who
is asking her to take a turn at the roller rink, a singer measures
her success by how captivated the audience becomes. The
responsive laughter during her patter between songs, the hushed
silences were all there. This woman was batting 1000.

But not with me. An internal voice was telling me, "Valerie
Bell, she is taking *your* turn around the rink."

If one could really be green with envy, as the expression
goes, then I was positively verdant and getting greener by the
second. If a soul mirror had been held up to my soul at that
moment, it would have revealed something horribly reptilian.
My emotions explored a subterranean level of my soul. There
my hardened heart clothed itself in an armor of scales no song
could penetrate. Cold-bloodedly I waited for the songstress to
end the torture so I could slink from the room before I had to
listen to anyone rave about how great she was.

Yes, just as that smart, little, green muppet Kermit sang—if
you have ever been envious, if you have ever been jealous, you
know, "It's not easy being green!" He was singing about skin coloring, but the soul does not wear that particular color well either.

So what was my problem? Please understand that from the
time I was a small girl, whether in our living room, on the plat-
form at church, or a stage at school, I have been singing. Writing is just an aberration of my middle years. No matter how
much I write, an internal voice whispers to me that I am really
a singer. I know what it is like to enter the musical dimension,
to soar and glide. It has to be the ultimate endorphin releaser. It

is a kind of flight, and it can be most addictive. To have to give up this experience to a younger or better singer can definitely produce withdrawal symptoms in an aging singer's life. I know.

My charming mother was the quintessential stage mother. She was convinced I was her singing daughter. From the time I could sing "Twinkle Twinkle Little Star," she was pushing me on people. Anyone who had an ear and a second was fair game. If the phone rang and it was a wrong number, my mother would hold the receiver up to my mouth and tell me to sing a few bars. If the mail carrier struggled through a storm, my mother would invite him in and then . . . "Oh by the way, I have a singing daughter. Would you like to hear her while you wait?"

The night I was baptized my mother concocted a surprise for my father, who was the church's music minister. I was just twelve years old. After I was baptized, instead of speaking my testimony, I sang it soaking wet, freezing cold, shaking with fear. "I Don't Have to Wait Until I'm Grown Up." I remember it as the most frightening event of my childhood. This was my mother's idea, and because she was not a musician, I doubt she ever considered what singing might be like under these unfavorable circumstances.

She formed my identity around singing. Losing singing was like losing self. Could she have ever known what a painful process music would set into place in my life?

Envy, the Suitor of Aging Women

Aging is, by its very nature, a process of loss. It is incredibly easy for envy to fill up the vacuum left by loss of beauty, potential, and identity. Successful aging requires redefinition of self at many crossroads in life. Fail to redefine, get stuck playing the tapes of loss in your mind, and negativity may become the defining characteristic of your "second half." Envy is the perverse suitor of the aging woman. Envy seeks women from the lonely, middle-aged shadows and asks, "Want to skate? Care to dance?" Check your dance card. Envy would like all your dances.

As I sat at that concert for broadcasters, I had to admit that I was definitely not flying nor was my journey Godward. Proverbs says that envy rots the bones, which perfectly describes the feeling I was experiencing. My soul was beginning to decompose, to decay.

Consider all the envious biblical characters who were willing to trade everything for that one turn around the rink—the turn that wasn't theirs. As a child, it was clear to me that they were the bad guys. I never identified with them. But as an adult, I recognize that unchecked jealousy or envy, no matter how subtle, aligns me with them. Envy makes me their kindred spirit. I was one of Joseph's siblings, standing over his prison pit, scheming how to get rid of father's favorite. I understood what compelled Sarah to cast a defenseless and pregnant Hagar, a pregnancy that resulted from Sarah's own scheming, into the wilderness to nearly certain death. I agreed with nagging, whining Martha that Jesus should make my sister Mary stop occupying his time and get in the kitchen to share my workload.

This was an ugly crowd, and I was running with it.

Envy Eats Our Hearts Out

The dictionary defines *envy* as the "painful or resentful awareness of an advantage enjoyed by another joined with a desire to possess the same advantage."

In other words, she has it; you want it.

Jealousy is a Siamese twin to envy, joined at the rotting bone, but with a slight twist. Jealousy is a fierce desire to protect an advantage you possess.

In other words, you have it; you want to keep it.

As in my case, we can suffer from both envy and jealousy at the same time, and so we may confuse the two and use them interchangeably. They are not the same.

Envy is the more dangerous of the twins. For centuries those who specialize in the care of the soul considered envy one of the seven deadly sins. Deadly to whom? Deadly to self. Envy is the cannibal of the soul. You might as well take your heart out and eat it bite by bilious bite.

> Envy feeds on itself, and is a sort of greed with a vengeance. Envy is destined to be in a perpetual state of longing, howling for what appears just out of reach like a shivering dog baying at the moon. Envy above all breeds more envy. Envy grows poor because others gain wealth; Envy grows sick because others are healthy; Envy grows gaunt watching others eat.[1]

Envy, the Source of Foolish Choices

When envy puts us on a path of self-destruction, it intends to make fools of us. Becoming perversely connected with another woman through envy, wanting what that other woman has, whether it is her turn around the rink, her opportunities, or nearly any other thing, however insignificant, her couch, her hair, her voice, can propel us toward foolish choices. Even if you have never been prone to gossip in your life, become envious of another woman and watch what happens. It becomes just a little too convenient to defame the name and the reputation of the person who is the object of our envy. Even better, if we can find someone who is struggling with resentment toward the same person. MEOW! Cat crossing! Watch the claws when envy has a foothold in a woman's life. Envy propels us toward foolish choices!

Envy can produce ultimate fools. Ultimate fools are the ones to whom envy has successfully masqueraded as love. I wonder how many homes have been broken, how many children have been left motherless or fatherless by those who mistook their lustful, envious desire to possess someone else's spouse as the love of the century. What a devastating shock to have traded in everything—home, reputation, family, jobs, relationship to God—only to realize it was not love after all, just an envious, empty trip around the rink. When the skating music dies down and the lights of reality come up, envious conquest, camouflaging as love, makes fools of many. She has it; you want it. Be careful when you hear the sound of that skating music. Envy's invitation to dance is a fool's party.

Envy Enlarges Our Evil Capacity

Envy also destroys our ability to connect with people, especially people whom we would normally admire. Envy builds ice fences of isolation. It deep-freezes the heart's capacity to love. It rejoices in others' losses and resents their joys. Envy is cold. We are never compassionate toward those we envy. We withhold love; we do not practice patient, kind love with someone to whom we are perversely attached through envy. We are so focused on their advantage, we do not feel their pain. We see those we envy one dimensionally. It enlarges our heart's capacity for evil toward others. Note these words from James 4:

> What causes fights and quarrels among you? Don't they come from your desires that battle within you? You want something but don't get it. You kill and covet, but you cannot have what you want. . . . Do you think Scripture

says without reason that the spirit he caused to live in us envies intensely? ... Submit yourselves, then, to God. Resist the devil, and he will flee from you. Come near to God and he will come near to you. Wash your hands, you sinners, and purify your hearts, you double-minded.... Humble yourselves before the Lord, and he will lift you up.

So envy is self-destructive; it propels us toward foolish choices; it separates us from others; it is the beginning of greater evils of the heart. That is pretty scary, but wait; there is still more—the worst impact of envy on our souls.

Envy Destroys the Perception of Our Own Lives

Perhaps the saddest result of all of envy's evil in our souls is that envy destroys our ability to love our own lives. That is because envy disturbs our perception of God's goodness. In the midst of enormous blessing, envy gives us the perverse capacity of feeling second fiddle, that we live with a lesser portion. When envy really has a hold on us, we do not even want what the other woman has; we want *better* than what she has. Envy is really sick!

A Look in the Mirror of Your Soul

The difficulty is owning up to having a problem with envy. We know it is ugly. But take a brave look into the mirror of your soul. Is something green and reptilian reflecting back to you? Not sure? Then try to honestly answer these questions. Is there another woman who keeps coming up derogatorily in conversations with a friend? Do you seem always to talk about a particular woman? Do you feel an unexplained distance between yourself and another woman? Do you feel delight when another woman fails or struggles? Would you like to see the score evened out in the life of someone whom you perceive as living with some advantage? Are you glad when another is sad, unhappy when she is happy? If you are courageous enough to be honest and you answer yes to any of those questions, you, too, may be traveling with the ugly, envious crowd. Your soul may be draped in green. Take it from Trevor the Terrible, "That color looks horrible on you."

Envy's Antidote

Take heart. There is an antidote to this soul cancer. Envy need not be terminal. It is checked by contentment. Thankfulness restores a healthy perspective about our lives.

A young couple shared how they learned about thankfulness from an older neighbor, Mr. Roth.

An old man showed up at the back door of the house we were renting. Opening the door a few cautious inches, we saw his eyes were glassy and his furrowed face glistened with silver stubble. He clutched a wicker basket holding a few unappealing vegetables. He bid us good morning and offered his produce for sale. We were uneasy enough to make a quick purchase to alleviate both our pity and our fear.

To our chagrin, he returned the next week, introducing himself as Mr. Roth, the man who lived in the shack down the road. As our fears subsided, we got close enough to realize that it wasn't alcohol, but cataracts, that marbleized his eyes. On subsequent visits, he would shuffle in, wearing two mismatched right shoes, and pull out a harmonica. With glazed eyes set on a future glory, he'd puff out old gospel tunes between conversations about vegetables and religion.

On one visit, he exclaimed, "The Lord is so good! I came out of my shack this morning and found a bag full of shoes and clothing on my porch."

"That's wonderful, Mr. Roth!" we said. "We're happy for you."

"You know what's even more wonderful?" he asked. "Just yesterday I met some people that could use them."[2]

A thankful heart has transforming power. It can make a poor man feel rich, rich enough to give things away! A thankful spirit can sustain a woman through the losses of health, beauty, relationships, potentiality, and wealth as she ages. Thankfulness is the medication of the spirit ... even when things are not good, you can still feel good! Someone has said, "God has been so lavish in his gifts that you can lose some priceless ones, the equivalent of whole kingdoms, and still be indecently rich."[3] Notice the focus of that statement. Thankfulness takes the sting out of life by focusing away from loss to those blessings which remain.

A Powerful, Transforming Prayer

In 1989 when I was diagnosed with malignant melanoma, my health was no longer guaranteed. I knew I could be in the process of losing everything. I definitely was not "laughing at the days to come." Life seemed incredibly fragile and insecure. My worst fears about dying concerned leaving my family in pain. Here was a heartbreak they might experience because of me. I could be the cause of their sorrow. I cried a lot during that initial month. It was as if I had been tenderized. I cried at sad things. I cried at beautiful things.

Nights were the worst. My fears would become irrational and overwhelming. I could not get to sleep; I could not stay asleep. *How come trouble keeps knocking on my door?* I thought of my friends who had their parents, who had their health. By comparison, they seemed to be coasting through life. I would never wish anything bad on them, but I certainly felt that my life stick had come up on the short end. I envied the ease and well-being with which they sailed through life.

In sad desperation one night I started praying. It was a different prayer. It wasn't a "heal me, save my life" prayer. Instead, it was a litany of thankfulness juxtaposed against my health.

Every sentence began, "I am a woman who has cancer." Not exactly a cheerful beginning, right? But then I would end the sentence with something about my life that I loved. It was simple. It sounded like this:

"I am a woman who has cancer. But my husband loves me and cares for me.

"I am a woman who has cancer. But my children are thriving.

"I am a woman who has cancer. But my friends can make me laugh."

No blessing was too small to be included. I had not even prayed like this for a week when the first part of the sentence became less interesting, boring even, when compared with clean sheets, spring flowers, purring kittens, a beautifully set table, and music. Something began to change. I started to feel less sick. I was still breathing, living well, and loving my life at the moment. God was good to Valerie Bell, even if she had cancer!

I believe the practice of this litany was key to restoring my sense of well-being. I began to see my life as normal, not cursed, but blessed even. I could not entertain those two opposing perspectives on life; I could not both be envious and blessed. I chose blessed.

But God's definition of thankfulness and mine are often a universe apart. God says we should give thanks in everything. I struggle with that. I think he could not mean that literally. I want to give thanks for the things that bring me joy and cause me happiness. When we thank God for sorrowful intruders, frustrating circumstances, or maddening relationships, we are indicating to God that we trust him to work out in our lives that which is best for us.

Thankfulness, a Powerful, Transforming Soul Tool

Thankfulness is not a child's verse at the supper table. It's not doll-like pilgrims decorating a festive, autumnal holiday table. The everyday practice of thankfulness is powerful, capable of changing our entire perspective on life. Thankfulness is what keeps our ships from going down when life's seas threaten to swamp us. It also helps us to realize the blessings we experience in the everyday nitty-gritty mundaneness of our lives.

For instance, I'm learning I can thank God for the dust in my home. You see, in my home dust is not just dust. It is the accumulating evidence of my lack of homemaking ability. It shakes a grimy finger at me and accuses me of neglect of my domestic responsibilities. Now, some women do not understand this struggle of mine. They are the ones who only have new dust in their homes, the kind that whisks off surfaces with a light swipe or feather duster. I do not have new dust in my home. My dust is old dust. Old dust becomes a part of the molecular structure of the surface it is covering. It becomes ingrained, gritty, sticky, and removable only by sandpaper.

But I am learning to look at my dust differently these days. A new perspective has taught me that if dust is covering my things, then I *have* things. Refugees do not worry about dust. Homeless people do not have rooms of things crying for attention. You and I have dust because we are prosperous, rich even, compared to many. Why do we take so much for granted? A grateful spirit can transform a house of burden into a home of blessing, a life of sadness into a life of blessing.

Another thing I am learning to be thankful for in these middle years is that for most of my life money has been tight. Looking back I am realizing how resourceful a person becomes when necessary.

I had a phone call that pointed this out to me. A woman, a very wealthy woman, had seen my picture in a magazine. I was in my (dusty) living room, which had been given a glow by the photographer's lens. Things looked antiqued, not just old. I was sitting on our ten-year-old couch. This well-to-do woman apologized for calling, but she needed my help. She loved my couch. She had been looking everywhere for it. Would I mind telling her where I had found it?

With a quick prayer that went something like, "Oh Lord, help me not to sin by enjoying this too much," I told the woman where I had found the couch.

"I bought that couch ten years ago at a drug and alcohol rehabilitation center in our area. It was donated by the manufacturer. It was quite reasonable, but I got the money even then by selling my old couch to a friend. The lamp in the picture was my mother's. The coffee table in the picture I found at a garage sale and ..."

The woman laughed on the other end. "I get the picture, Valerie. No wonder I couldn't find that couch anywhere. I'm shopping in the wrong places!"

Short on money? Be thankful. You may become resourceful and creative. You will learn to make beautiful one-of-a-kind things with your hands. No money will be able to buy the cross-stitch that hangs on your walls or the furniture you have restored or the curtains you have sewn.

As we age we experience many losses. A wise woman will focus on the small blessings of her life as a way of loving her life and keeping her losses in perspective. Learn to appreciate what you cannot lose: the air, the sun, the love of God, a constant friend, and a new day. Nurture a contented soul.

A friend of mine once prayed, "Lord, help me not to want anything you don't have for me." I recognized her prayer as an excellent check on the tendency to lace up my skates and take a turn around the rink with envy. Now, when I hear the skating music, I whisper that prayer. I thank God for my life and my loves.

Thankfulness transforms skating music into a spiritual song:

> *And now let the weak say I am strong.*
> *Let the poor say I am rich,*
> *Because of what the Lord has done for us.*
> *Give thanks.*[4]

Seven

Red-Hot Mamas
I've Known and Been

"Conversation indeed" said the Rocket. "You have talked the whole time yourself. That is not conversation."

"Somebody must listen" answered the Frog, "and I like to do all the talking myself."

"You are a very irritating person" said the Rocket, "and very ill bred. I hate people who talk about themselves, as you do, when one wants to talk about oneself, as I do . . ."

—Oscar Wilde, "The Remarkable Rocket"

[Love] does not boast, it is not proud. It is not rude.

—1 Corinthians 13:4–5

Some women you never forget. They stick! My friend was like that. She was a Red-Hot Mama, a peacock among women. Beautiful and charming, she attracted attention with her flashy beauty and effervescent personality. There was no ignoring her. Her lipstick was always just a little too bright. Her laughter regularly broke the sound barrier. Her hair was bleached to bombshell blond. Her cleavage spilled over the low-cut necklines she wore with an apologetic air that declared, "Well, if you've got it, you've just got it!" This woman's lactation equipment could make Dolly Parton blush!

She consistently wore big, flashy hats even when they were not in style. Those wide, floppy rims were her backdrops, her stage settings, the props for the main show: her expressive eyes. I had to admit, her eyes were enchanting. She could make them dance and cast spells. I had often watched them as they widened in conversation. Her eyes could make you feel as if you were the all-time great conversationalist—witty, urbane, clever. Even if you had only said something mundane and ordinary like, "Looks like it could rain today," she would look at you as if you were especially clever and insightful. She would fasten her eyes on you and purr something back like, "Well, aren't you the amazing one to notice!"

Men loved her. Oh, they acted as if they did not. They would speak of her with disclaimers, but mostly they loved her . . . that male-ego stroking thing, you know. Needless to say, she was slightly more popular and accepted in the male crowd than she was among her female acquaintances. But if she missed the camaraderie of her sisters, she never let on. She never seemed to notice the bristling of some man's wife when she pinched his cheek and cooed, "Oh, you're sooooo adorable!" She never seemed to hear the meow when she left the rest of the women in the room to their own less formidable attention-getting devices and surrounded herself with her adoring male friends. She oozed a kind of sensuality that promised things that had not been experienced since the Garden of Eden. Mm . . . Mm . . . Mm!

She was a Red-Hot Mama!

Actually, I have to admit that I kind of liked, even enjoyed the woman. I knew it was naughty of me, but I just enjoyed watching how other people navigated the social waves she made. How often I chuckled at the discomfort playing on some poor man's face at her unsubtle overtures, or at the dismay of some female accustomed to the spotlight, who suddenly found herself yanked to the curtains while my friend performed her eyebrow-raising, scene-stealing, upstaging routine.

A Little Red-Hot Mama in Me, a Little in You

I never was sure why my friend behaved in such an overt way. Did some terrible hole of the soul drive her to such unseemly behavior? Or maybe it was not as deep as that; maybe she just lacked social savvy. I could not be sure. But the amazing thing is that through the years, I have noticed a little of the Red-Hot Mama in me, and I have noticed a little of the Red-Hot Mama in many others. I have come to realize that my friend was just a more blatant variation of a feminine theme many of us display.

Have I lost you? If you are protesting, "Come on, I couldn't be more different than the woman you just described!" let me remind you that you do not have to be blatantly sensual to be a Red-Hot Mama. Most of us have refined our attention-getting behavior to a more subtle level.

For instance, have you ever found yourself dropping things into conversations that, subtly of course, let people know your station in life?

For me it might go this way. "Oh, in my last book I wrote about . . . (surprised pause making space for those words to sink in). Oh you didn't know? Why yes . . . I am an AUTHOR." It is important to emphasize the word *author*. It carries so much more clout than *writer*. I mean a writer could be anyone, from the person who writes the copy for the back of cereal boxes to someone who writes obituaries. Author! That's the clout carrier!

Can't relate? Well, maybe you have noticed this little tendency. Someone has just told an adorable anecdote about their children, some cute thing they said or did. Before the laughter dies down, you just happen to remember something your child did that was just a little cuter or funnier, so of course you tell your better-than-the-next-woman's story. You shove her from the spotlight, steal her stage marks, and shine, shine, shine!

We play the Red-Hot Mama in a lot of ways. If someone tells a joke, you know a funnier one.

If someone is worried, you are experiencing full-blown panic attacks.

If someone is ill, you are dying!

Ever notice what happens when two "Queens of Cheap" get together? You know the kind of woman I am talking about, the woman with reverse snobbery who brags about all the bargains she finds. They can be wearing the same blouse, but if one of them brags about buying it at TJ Maxx for nine bucks, you can be sure the other one found it at the Salvation Army Surplus Store for two, and will let her know!

Sometimes a Red-Hot Mama plays the role of the answer woman. You will recognize this woman. She is the woman who knows everything. She is mother superior to the world. She always has the last word in conversations, like the ultimate human punctuation point. You have seen this happen before. Everyone is sympathetically wrestling over a problem. The idea is to empathize, show concern, and care for a sister who is hurting. Enter the answer woman. Bang! She knows exactly what needs to happen to resolve the problem. End of conversation. She places herself on a pedestal of wisdom from which she can look down on the rest of struggling womankind. Always knowledgeable, always insightful, full of self-importance, this Red-Hot

Mama intimidates with a pseudo-intellectualism that beats other women down to their "proper" place ... anywhere beneath her!

Just kind of sets off the gag reflex, doesn't it? And yet, how many times do I catch myself playing the answer woman version of the Red-Hot Mama?

Love Refines the Red-Hot Mama Routine

Now, besides being totally socially ridiculous, the problem with being a Red-Hot Mama is that there is little room for love in a woman who is taken up with herself. This is the major soul flaw of Red-Hot Mamas. When we play the Red-Hot Mama we are determined to project *self*. We boast, we are proud and exceedingly rude with our interrupting, ignoring, and outshining of others. Have you noticed how a Red-Hot Mama will do practically anything to be noticed and have center-front stage? There she is, vaunting, flaunting, and behaving unseemly! Some women know exactly why we are willing to upstage, outshine, and beat them down. They know we are full of self. A Red-Hot Mama's soul mirror is full of self.

Here's how one sociologist describes the Red-Hot Mama phenomena:

> In informal conversation, the self-oriented person repeatedly seeks to turn attention to himself. ... This "conversational narcissism" is the key manifestation of the dominant attention-getting psychology in America. It occurs in informal conversations among friends, family and co-workers. The profusion of popular literature about listening and the etiquette of managing those who talk constantly about themselves suggests its pervasiveness in every day life; its contemporary importance is indicated by the early appearance of these problems in the most

recent edition of Emily Posts' etiquette manual. . . . In observations of ordinary conversations, I have found a set of extremely common conversational practices which show an unresponsiveness to others' topics and involve turning them into one's own.[1]

The Red-Hot Mama takes on a more chilling perspective when viewed through not just a sociological but a spiritual grid.

Vanity is one way pride shows up. Holding the center of attention—one's own and others'—is almost the meaning of life to some of us. Body-builders sculpt their flesh, intent on the mirror as they lift weights. A priest offers the perfect liturgy, every tone and gesture immaculate, the congregation serving as mirror. . . . Pride also shows up in its effect on one's relation with other creatures, for the self-centered, other people do not easily make an impression; nothing besides the self has very much reality. The husband who expects his wife to attend to his creature comforts and puts up with her prattle only because he can filter it out is really married to himself.

When I was growing up an elderly relative occasionally made a pontifical visitation to our home. . . . The children paid her court, if they knew what was good for them. She was not a tyrant, simply the hub of reality.

It is in relation to God, of course, that pride . . . takes its most vicious turn. The self-deification that is implicit in other forms of pride here becomes explicit. The self is god.[2]

Here is the beauty of God's plan for the development of our feminine souls: He intended that love would have a refining effect on the Red-Hot Mama inside us. The love of God, active in our life, quiets ego's attempts to shout, "Notice me! Adore me!" Love rubs away the rough edges of self-promotion with interest in others. Love is polite and gracious. No one ever feels beat up when she meets a reformed Red-Hot Mama who has learned to stop using others like a projection screen for the story of her own life.

There Is Nothing Like Being Around Another Red-Hot Mama to Bring It Out in Yourself

I was almost a Red-Hot Mama the other day. Let me assure you, I have been one hundreds of times before, the only difference was, this time I caught myself. I was flying from the West Coast to Chicago, trying to make conversation with the woman seated next to me. She could not have been less interested. Although she was not a flashy dresser like my friend with the hats—in fact she was rather dumpy—I realized after asking a few conversation starters and having none asked back, that she simply was not feeling social. I suspected she had sized me up fairly quickly, saw my sweatsuit and cross-stitch in hand, and figured she was sitting next to a dull, little housewife.

Oh, she was condescending enough to talk about herself, however. And how fascinating four hours of that was! That's when I began to suspect she was a Red-Hot Mama. She told me she was a professor at one of the major state universities ... Dr. Somebody. She spoke clearly and slowly as if she thought I was mentally disabled and more than likely unable to understand her advanced vocabulary. She acted as if I bored her to tears and informed me that this plane ride (not in her usual first-class seat) was a distasteful experience. There was no doubt about it, I was being snubbed. Who did she think she was? This was no peacock among women. The nerve! This mousy, owlish woman complete with navy blue suit and bun was snubbing Valerie Bell, Author!

Well, there is nothing like being around another Red-Hot Mama to bring it out in you! When she told me she was publishing a book about the history of turkey processing, I wanted to jiggle my head, smirk, and say something sarcastic like . . . "Well, I bet that'll be a best-seller!"

When she looked down her nose at me and declared, "You know, in the academic world it's publish or perish." I wanted to shove down her little turkey neck that I knew about publishing, that I was an author too, for pete's sake! I was not writing academic gibberish either. No! No! No! I was writing spiritual, life-altering, world-changing stuff! I wanted to pluck her little feathers and tell her who I was. I wanted to strut my stuff and one-up her, so that she would know she was sitting next to SOMEBODY!

Later, when I told this story to my sons, they said, "We hope you gave it to her, Mom!" They expressed my feelings exactly. I wanted to give the big "A" word, *author*, right back at her. But an inner voice told me to be still. I was to be quiet and learn. So I submitted to a new discipline of not always having to project myself on others. I listened. I asked questions. I made supportive sounds like, "Uh-huh, really?" (I avoided Gobble! Gobble! Gobble! and Balk! Balk! Balk! although I wondered if she would have noticed if I had interjected them in her monologue.) For the duration of a very long flight, I listened to the fascinating details of turkey processing since the 1900s.

When it was time to leave, she never said a word of good-bye or looked back. During the entire flight she had never said one gracious personal word to me or asked me a question. I was a nobody to her, just as I had been nobody to her at the beginning of our trip. I was simply someone on whom to project herself. Yes, I felt I had been snubbed. But I had also learned a lot about graciousness and the love that comes from God that helps us all to live beyond self-interest to loving (even if it is only in passing) others as we should. Sometimes love takes the backseat, surrenders the spotlight, smiles in the shadows, and learns all about turkey processing.

Self, the Soul's Slaver

If envy is the cannibal of the soul, then self is soul's slaver. A woman taken up with self is bound with the chains of her own self-preoccupation. Fetters of self-interest and manacles of self-projection prevent her from the very thing she most longs to experience, connection with other people. Why do we play the Red-Hot Mama? I have a theory. I believe our vauntings of self are actually desperate attempts to connect. Our behavior screams, "Here I am; notice me!" but our inappropriate assaults counter our need to connect. In the end, we repulse rather than attract others. Perhaps my airplane Red-Hot Mama was not snubbing me but trying desperately and awkwardly to connect.

Just a few months after my mother's death, we moved from South Florida, where my husband had been on the staff of a large church. With that move I lost my identity as a pastor's wife. I also lost my support systems that would have helped me carry my grief over losing my last parent. My sense of being lost was compounded, because I had not yet developed the appropriate social skills needed to be a layperson. As a pastor's family, we were always included, always invited. Everyone knew us. Suddenly no one knew me. No one invited. No one included. I found myself trying to explain to people who I was, who I had been, and why I felt so sad. But actually, when I boiled it all down, I was talking about me a lot. I had never felt so disconnected in my life! I was playing the Red-Hot Mama, repulsing instead of attracting, trying desperately to connect and managing instead to miss nearly everyone I met. The problem with being a Red-Hot Mama is that you end up with only yourself for comfort. It is a formula for utter loneliness.

Isolation, an Increasing Problem with Age

Are isolation and disconnectedness problems for women as they age? You bet! Big time!

In 1995, Chicago experienced the second hottest summer in recorded history. Combined with high humidity, it was definitely the most uncomfortable summer. Worst of all, it also was the most deadly.

More than seven hundred people died in July alone when homes became ovens as the temperatures day after day soared past one hundred degrees. It was headline news. Then in late August the papers ran another front-page, heat-related article. It told a story of another kind of human suffering. The pictures showed a 6-foot-deep and 160-foot-long trench lined with sixty-eight plain wood caskets. These were the forgotten victims of Chicago's record-setting heat wave. It was a mass paupers' grave like something we expect to see only in war-torn countries or lands decimated by plagues. But this was Chicago, right in the heartland of America! Even though an intense search had been made for relatives or friends, no one had claimed these sixty-eight bodies. These people had absolutely no human connections! No one mourned or attended their funerals. No one wept for them. There were no flowers, no condolence cards, no casseroles delivered to grieving relatives, no kind, personal words publicly spoken, no eulogies, no remembrances. They were mostly older people. The papers reported, "They were buried much like the way they had lived their final years: alone."[3]

How utterly sad! At some point these people were all connected. They undoubtedly had parents, siblings, relatives, and neighbors. But through the years bridges burn, relationships break, we lose those with whom we would most naturally connect. Without appropriate skills that help us connect to others, that help us counteract the process of loss in life, we all face a potentially lonely future.

The feminine soul is a social soul. But with inappropriate behavior, we thwart our own need to connect. I watched a group of older women playing cards one night. The "girls" had gathered. I listened to the girl talk. It was truly revealing. Is this what I am becoming? I wondered. They all talked simultaneously. No one listened. They did not even bother to respond to each other's comments. Balk! Balk! Balk! Gobble! Gobble! Gobble! It was funny to me at the time, but since I have wondered if all those older women went home that night feeling more isolated, more alone, more disconnected than they were when they came. They were definitely Red-Hot Mamas. They upstaged each other; they outshone each other; they grabbed each other from the spotlight. But beneath the talk and the posturing and the noise, they were lonely, aging women, trying desperately to connect but managing to distance themselves further with every self-projected word.

Are you a Red-Hot Mama, trying desperately to connect but feeling more isolated and lonely all the time? Have you developed a deep disinterest in other people so that anything they speak about is as interesting as turkey processing?

Or maybe you have stopped trying. You have begun to withdraw from other people. You are exhausted by your attempts to connect and tired of feeling repulsed. You feel sad and alone.

How to Connect Lovingly with Other People

There is a way out of loneliness. Learn to connect by drawing out other people. Stop the practice of constantly projecting yourself and allow other people the grace of talking about themselves. Believe me, you will be popular. You will be sought out. You will be mourned when you die.

Try this experiment for one day. For twenty-four hours do not talk about yourself. Do not talk about your children either. Do not talk about the books you've written or the mountains you've climbed. Edit name-dropping as well. For this experiment all the above are considered extensions of self. Are you able to connect without talking about yourself or without trying to impress other people? If you find an enormous hole, fill the conversational vacuum with interesting questions about the people you meet. Take the backseat. Early in her career Barbara Walters wrote a substantial book with a catchy title: *How to Talk with Practically Anybody about Practically Anything*. Page after page, one of the world's most celebrated interviewers gives advice that really boils down to one ploy: Ask questions; get other people talking about themselves.

I suggest you try it for just twenty-four hours: Let someone else shine in the spotlight. Enjoy helping some other Red-Hot Mama feel connected, if only for a few minutes. Make it a habit and, in time, your phone will be ringing, your doorbell will be sounding, you will be sharing life with others again.

Love is the great life connector; it liberates the aging feminine soul from self. It frees the soul from self-obsession. It banishes narcissism from reflecting in the mirrors of our souls. Love allows the patient kindness of listening and attention to others to mark our lives. Allowing others to shine is a great gift we can give to a lonely, disconnected world. It is also a grace that allows our souls to connect appropriately to others. It may not always be easy, but it is always right.

.   I feel a little chagrined. I think I was too hard on the turkey woman, Dr. Somebody. Looking back, I realize I, too, made some snap judgments. I'll probably never see her again. But who knows? Maybe we'll run into each other again in the friendly skies sometime. Of course, maybe you'll see her before I do. You'll know her immediately. Tight little bun. Navy suit. Talks about turkey processing. If you see her, will you do me a favor? Do what I should have done, what I'd like another opportunity to do. Smile and mean it. Be kind and find out everything you can about turkey processing. Reach across the awkward divide and give a lonely woman a few hours of belonging and friendship. And if you remember it, tell her that Valerie Bell, housewife and cross-stitcher, said hi.

Eight

Club Snob

Humility means a refusal to do the final judging about who is "in" and who is "out." God will someday separate the tares from the wheat. Until that day comes we must approach every encounter with our fellow human beings with the awareness that the Lord is "slow to anger and abounding in steadfast love and faithfulness."

—Richard J. Mouw, *Uncommon Decency*

Love seeketh not her own.

—1 Corinthians 13:5 (KJV)

$\mathcal{U}$nder certain conditions, the feminine soul has a problem with shrinkage. I learned this at "Maison de Froufrou" when I was eavesdropping on other people's conversations. Now in my own defense, let me assure you that I am not aggressive in this pursuit. You might say unsolicited pieces of conversations somehow manage to float into my ears and onto my page! That is exactly what happened in this particular incident. Really!

Here is the scene: It was a typical, blustery, bitter Chicago January day: the month of the year when I question why I live in this city, the month of the year when I think Chicago should be legally closed. My husband was fortunate enough to be in West Palm Beach, Florida, speaking for a pastor's conference. I was not invited. The thought of him enjoying tropical breezes and warm, sunny days without me grieved my wifely heart. Fortunately for me, it was also his birthday, so I had a perfect excuse. When his meetings were over, Happy Birthday, there I would be!

A short plane ride later, and I had left winter behind me. For the occasion, just in case there would be a little problem with my presumptuousness, I had attempted a Queen Esther imitation. Perfumed, oiled, and coifed, dressed in glittery things, it was a middle-aged effort that I hoped would remind him of why he married me. He bought it!

I had asked local friends to recommend a special restaurant to celebrate this milestone. They told me about "Maison de Froufrou," a restaurant on Worth Avenue in West Palm Beach. They also advised that we go at lunchtime unless we wanted to take out a second mortgage on our home to pay for the evening dinner prices. This was going to be a memorable experience!

It did not take us long to realize that we had never eaten in such a place. Oh, we'd eaten in other restaurants where the atmosphere was lovely, the tablecloths and flowers fresh. We had just never been treated like this by waiters before. They acted like tuxedoed automatons. They never showed a flicker of personality. It made you wonder if real blood ran through their veins or if they were battery operated. All our requests were answered with stock replies like, "I will attend to it immediately, madam," or "That will be no inconvenience at all, sir."

About halfway through the meal, we realized why they seemed so robotic. This was a place the extremely wealthy frequented regularly; most of the patrons were not once-in-a-lifetime drop-ins, like Steve and me. The waiters had been trained to behave like servants. They were not to cozy up to the customers, because they were not to presume to be on the same social plane. They were beneath their rich patrons and were to act accordingly. They were to be as unobtrusive, as unnoticeable, as "not there" as possible.

Well, well, well! Wasn't this a quaint societal practice, a little leftover from the days of that charmer, Marie Antoinette, no doubt. Amazingly, the young waiters carried it off straight-faced. I thought they deserved Academy Awards for not laughing in the faces of their take-themselves-oh-so-seriously patrons. They must have been well paid to be willing to act out this untruth. But what kind of people would expect others to act dehumanized, blank-faced, and servile?

I began to look around at the other tables. Everyone appeared to have just breezed in from a morning on the family yacht. They were all in "play clothes" a la Ralph Lauren. Casual chic prevailed. Apparently everyone's name was "darling" or "dear." Newcomers who joined the group were greeted with kisses on both cheeks. This was the Lake Wobegon crowd in reverse—all the women were beautiful, all the men were tan, and all the children were most likely at boarding school! My Queen Esther routine was way over the top for this idle rich crowd! But even as I sensed that Steve and I were definitely out of place, another stronger, more urgent, pressing feeling prevailed.

Curiosity!

Who were these people? Why were they acting like characters from an F. Scott Fitzgerald novel? Great Gatsbys! I could not have been more curious if dinosaurs had walked in the front door, seated themselves next to me, placed linen napkins in their laps, and ordered from the menu! In a way, I suspected these people might actually *be* dinosaurs left over from some predemocratic era in history.

In no time, my ears had joined the next table over. I couldn't help but hear the conversation. Mr. Tanned-For-Life was leading a discussion about the C. S. Lewis movie they had seen the night before. *Maybe this 100-percent virgin cotton crowd was not so different from me after all.* I had seen that same movie the night before as well—probably in the same theater. But as they discussed the meaning of the movie, I realized, somewhat to my delight, that much of it had gone right over their heads.

I was not able to enjoy feeling smug for long, however.

Mr. Tanned-For-Life lowered his voice. He spoke directly to the woman to his left, the one with the face tucked so tightly that her skin looked like plastic wrap stretched over last week's leftovers. They were sharing a secret, something they did not want to be heard talking about. This I had to hear! He leaned toward her, I leaned toward them, and then in a whisper, edged in disdain, *it* floated into my ears, "But, my dear, the *element* at the theater last night ... darling! They were absolutely *N.O.K.!*"

I do not remember where I learned this, but somehow I knew exactly what he was saying. It was snob talk, a kind of coded language some extremely wealthy people use when they do not want others to know what is being said. "The element" was a derogatory way of referring to the people who were in the theater, the people like me who had been at the movies last night. They say "element" when they mean "riffraff." N.O.K. is an abbreviation for Not Our Kind!

You Don't Have to Be Rich to Be a Snob

So be careful little eavesdropping ears what you hear! Strangely, I, a member of the "element" from the theater the night before, did not feel rejected. What was I feeling? A little shocked. Somewhat repulsed. Amused. As if I had caught someone doing something naughty. As we left the restaurant, their words rang in my ears as a warning against the exclusivity of my own heart. You see, you do not have to be rich to be a snob. There are a lot of poor snobs, believe me. You just need to buy into the concept that the world is comprised of two kinds: "us" and "them."

I once heard Carl Sandburg interviewed. He was asked which word he thought was the worst in the English language. He paused for a moment. I wondered which of all the vast horrible word possibilities this skilled wordsmith might choose. War? Hatred? Violence? He surprised me. He said he believed *exclusivity* is the worst word in our language. His comment has haunted me, and through the years, I have come to see his point. An exclusive, superior mind-set is what fuels wars and everyday hatreds. It is the source of so much that is destructive and dehumanizing in life. An exclusive soul—practiced in prejudice and superiority—is an ugly soul, shrunken and withered, an unfeeling, judgmental raisin, where a compassionate heart was meant to beat.

Club Snob Family-Style

Exclusive clubs of the heart, snob clubs, can be based on any cherished similarity: age, social strata, wealth, beauty, faith, even genetics. "Family only" is a particularly offensive snob club. It wounds those who are already wounded from not belonging.

Carolyn Stradley learned this as an eleven-year-old. Her mother died that year, and her father—though still in the community—had long ago left her and her slightly older brother to fend for themselves in their cabin in the mountains of north-eastern Georgia. She describes her utterly lonely life:

No one really cared. Everybody knew about me living alone and no one really cared. An Aunt once told me, "There's no way I'm going to take care of someone else's child while your Daddy is making good money and blowing it on a whore." Pardon me, but that's the way it was, and that was the attitude of the community. He was making good money and I was his responsibility, not theirs.

One Christmas—I guess I was about 11 or 12—I had been by myself, even my brother was gone. So I thought, "Well, it's Christmas Day, and there's gonna be good spirit and good cheer at the preacher's house." I walked across the field, crossed the creek on a footlog, and then back up through another field to his house. When I went in I didn't feel any kind of uncomfortableness. Their house was so nice and warm, and I was cold. I didn't have a fire at my house that day, and I was wet, on my way over I had slipped off the footlog and fallen down into the creek, just like a kid will. The smells of turkey and dressing and all that food had my mouth watering. You've got to look at an eleven-year-old kid to understand what I'm saying. Anyway I went in and the only thing I could think was, "Oh boy, I'm going to get something to eat because they wouldn't dare ask me to leave on Christmas Day. There's just no way."

And then all the family went in to eat. I stood back because I would never go into anyone's kitchen without being asked. Then the pastor came out and pulled me aside and he told me, "Carolyn, I don't get to spend much time with my family alone, and I would prefer to have this time alone. I would appreciate it if you could come back later." He didn't say, "Would you leave?" He said, "Come back later," but I knew what he meant. I'll tell you what. That was probably the only man I ever hated in my life. That man was an A-number-one hypocrite. I disliked him then, and I dislike him today, and he's dead. I still dislike anyone who even looks like him. I've had drunk guys in Atlanta come and try to rape me and I've fought them off with a butcher knife. I don't hate them the way I hate that preacher because they never professed to be loving and gentle and kind and then turn around and turn someone away.

I think that if it had not been for my faith in Jesus Christ as being my friend, I probably would have died.[1]

Carolyn did not die. She managed to survive an incredibly lonely childhood. This story is chilling, and not because a particularly great evil was brought against this young girl; what is so scary is that the pastor's response was both so easy and so devastating. It is an understandable mistake, yet it had such a wounding impact. You do not have to be evil to kill someone else's spirit, just someone whose personal holiday agenda fails to live up to the things publicly preached. Carolyn is right. That is hypocrisy. Even as a little girl she was offended by the gap in this man's stated beliefs and his actual practice.

Club Snob Church-Style

A man once told me about his experience growing up as one child of nine in a migrant-worker family. On Sundays his mother would manage to dress up the children and take them to church.

They never went in. They would sit on the outside front steps and listen to the beautiful music. Too uncomfortable to join the congregation and take a place in the pews, week after week they would sit on the outside. They were afraid they were N.O.K.—Not Our Kind—and, sadly, no one ever insisted differently.

Imagine having a hunger for God but finding yourself treated as "them," not "us" by God's people! Members of Church Club Snob will tell you that Jesus loves you but also remind you to remember your place and try not to cozy up to those who are your betters.

These days your ears do not have to walk very far in the Christian community to hear snob talk. In some Christian circles "us" and "them" talk is public and bold, broadcast on radio and television, not discreetly whispered and under the breath so as not to be offensive to the "element." No sensitivity is shown to the possibility of giving great, unforgiving offense. Understanding who is "in" and who is "out" and treating people appropriately is a basis for club membership. There is no pretense of reaching out to others; instead, club members are told to build moats around themselves and their families to keep isolated and pure from "them." Welcome to club snob, Christian-style!

Be careful of the clubs you join, the messages you buy into. If you are not being encouraged to appropriately relate to those outside the faith, but instead are encouraged to put on your "Onward Christian Soldier" boots and trample everyone who disagrees with your values, be careful! If the attitude is one of exclusivity and isolation, if "us" and "them" talk prevails instead of Christlike compassion and inclusiveness, if anger and a mean, judgmental spirit prevails, beware! Would Jesus run with the Christian club you have joined? Be careful of the company you keep. Snob clubs deform and shrink the soul.

To Jesus, No One Is N.O.K.

Scripture says the most excellent way is one in which love "seeketh not her own." Cherished similarities are not the basis for membership in the heart of a woman who has real soul. Love is given, love is lavished on others because of the character of the loving, mature soul, not because of the worth or value or cherished similarities of the lavished other. You only have to look at Jesus to see how opposite an us-and-them attitude is from his style of relating to those unlike himself. The inclusive approach to other people is where Jesus shone. Jesus' approach to women is particularly unique and exceedingly wonderful. He was that rare man who was comfortable with women. Jesus did not seek his own. To Jesus, no one is N.H.K., Not His Kind.

The woman at the well was his kind. She was the town floozy, probably a prostitute. She was the kind of woman respectable men never rode an elevator with, or traveled with in cars, or closed their office doors behind when she came in for counseling, afraid that something about her might rub off on them. Jesus didn't distance himself from her as if she were some kind of gender leper. Right out in bold, bald daylight, where anyone who wanted to could have watched and spread gossip about him, he initiated conversation. A more important priority than his reputation pressed Jesus to speak to her. Although she was far from respectable, Jesus apparently sensed that this woman was not far from the kingdom; when he turned the conversation to spiritual things, she was immediately interested in and engaged by his words.

Now notice the contrast when the disciples—the regular guys, so to speak—entered the scene in progress. They took one look and sized it up immediately. In a second, they knew what kind of woman she was. It makes you wonder if she was wearing a T-shirt that bragged, "So many men, so little time!" or something. Amazing! Maybe she was the Samaritan version of the Red-Hot Mama, a take-one-glance, engage-the-testosterone, ignite-the-libido babe. Whatever it was about her, it was blatant and immediately obvious. N.O.K., they thought. Oh, the disciples were careful not to verbalize their concerns. The text in John 4 states "no one asked." Their thoughts, however, are recorded: "Why are you talking with her?" The Disciple Snob Club thought her inappropriate even to speak with. But then, they were lesser men than Jesus.

Who Is "In" and Who Is "Out" in Your Spiritual Club?

Floozies and tax collectors, lepers and sinners were all Jesus' kind. Scripture records the disapproving "Tsk! Tsk! Tsk!" from the religiously correct of the day. Publicans! Sinners! How inappropriate, how gauche! Hypocrites, lesser sisters, lesser brothers always need to be highly aware of who is "in" and who is "out." When true spirituality is absent, faux spirituality requires external indications about club membership. You are "in" according to the do's and don'ts to which you subscribe. The club's bylaws become *the* bible, the test of club membership. Passion for the bylaws always overshadows passion for God or other people in spiritual snob clubs. Spiritual snob clubs shrivel the soul through exclusivity.

Be careful of the clubs you join. Some will make you feel kosher and religiously correct, but all the time your heart is becoming more exclusive and shrunk, your soul tutored in judgmental hypocrisy.

A Formula for Loneliness As You Age

I wonder, what does it take to get into your club? Asked another way, how do other people get a piece of your heart?

Have you noticed, as I have, a tendency as you age to edit your associations to a more homogenous and smaller group? The aging feminine soul must work against this tendency of drawing an ever-smaller circle of intimacy. Age naturally seeks comfort from that which is known, but ultimately it works against itself. A circle of exclusive friends drawn too close to the aging self is a sure formula for loneliness. If women exclusively seek their own as they mature, their souls revert to a condition of second pubescence, a kind of middle school cliquishness based on seeking our own. It is a condition of heart-childishness that some wear unaware of its inappropriateness. It is the aging growth pattern of lesser men and women.

My First Girlfriend—A Model for Successful Aging

I was fortunate to have almost the opposite experience from Carolyn Stradley when I was growing up. At three years of age, I had a girlfriend. She was the "girl" next door, and she had to be eighty if she was a day. She was the first truly old person I had met. I had to overcome my initial awe-filled fear of her wrinkled, bent, translucent blue-veined body. I was already age-prejudiced at three years old! From the ugly stepmothers of Cinderella to the old woman in Hansel and Gretel, older women of children's literature were stereotypically evil. I strongly considered that she might be a witch. Fortunately, she was closer to being a saint. My childhood prejudice about age did not hold up to this charming woman.

Although I was an everyday pest, I never remember being asked to come back later. She wooed me with shredded wheat and gingerbread men. She had a repertoire of incredibly sad stories that were sweetened by faith in God. She was an "in-your-face" believer; her faith was articulated right up front. I never had to wonder where she stood on anything, including my own behavior. She did not hesitate to scold me when I was naughty. She knew where to draw the line! She was involved enough with me that she was concerned about my character development and my spiritual journey. I learned to love her. I often took my naps in her big iron bed, right next to her. Even then, she did not send me away but included me. She was more than a wrinkled, old woman. To me she was beautiful, the first female friend of my heart.

My first girlfriend will always be my model for beauty in old age. When I was about seven or eight, she died. I mourned a woman who did not seek her own. I mourned a woman who was inclusive enough to make me feel as though I were in her club. I mourned a woman who cared enough to draw the line when I was wrong and love me at the same time. Though it has been more than forty years since we were neighbors, she continues to impact my vision of what a Christian woman ideally can be: an inclusive and caring soul; a woman who not only states what she believes but also becomes involved in other people's spiritual journeys; a woman who is winsome and beautiful even while covered with age spots and topped with snowy hair.

She loved me to Jesus by seeking me as her own.

"Isn't a Woman Here Who Isn't a Sinner in God's Eyes!"

I will never forget another old woman who showed us younger ones the way to open our hearts and souls to someone who was N.O.K. I was to speak for a women's retreat, but when the weekend came, I found myself struggling with a bad case of laryngitis. I sounded like Froggie. How could I talk all weekend? This was going to be disastrous!

God had other plans. During one of the sessions, just before I was to speak, a young woman, a new Christian, gave her testimony. As a teenager this woman was totally unchurched. When very young she became pregnant, married the father of her child (a young sailor), and moved far from her family. Her husband was abusive and angry at her for becoming pregnant. She delivered her first child, but too soon she was pregnant again. Her husband was furious. He threatened her. He threatened her child. He was insistent that this baby be aborted. She tried to protest and protect her unborn child, but she was no match for his anger and threats that became violent.

Put yourself in this young woman's place. You are telling your story to a large group of conservative Christian women. You are telling them about aborting a child you wanted. She must have strongly felt that she was N.O.K. When she tried to say the "A" word—*abortion*—she could not pronounce it. She literally choked on the word. She was the picture of shame. She hung her head, covered her face with her hands, and silently wept shame-filled, regret-filled, embarrassed tears.

It was awkward and quiet while we anxiously waited for her to compose herself and continue. Instead, her tears became sobs. Then in this intense moment from the back of the room, a well-worn, far-traveled old woman's voice spoke up, "We know what you're trying to say, darlin'. Isn't a woman here who isn't a sinner in God's eyes. It's okay. We understand and God forgives."

In a second, God's arms, in twenty different female versions—old and young, black and white and several shades in between, skinny and fat, flabby and firm—went around that sad young woman in the biggest group hug I had ever seen. They cried with her; they laughed with her. We prayed and praised God for his love and forgiveness. There was no doubt, those church women knew they were sinners each and every one. But they also knew something else. They knew they were God's friends, and they recognized another friend of God's when they saw her. Club initiation among the true friends of Jesus is incredibly sweet.

To the feminine soul who is a friend of God's, no one is N.O.K. There was no need to worry about speaking that day. With only what can amount to a kind of protective, divine irony, they never got around to me in that session anyway. Honestly? It was one of my best sessions ever!

What does it take to get into your club? Practice exclusivity and you are actually having the audacity to say to Jesus, "Some of your friends just aren't good enough for me! Sorry, but I am too busy being kosher to be caring!"

Join the Christian Sorority of Caring

Christian women who have had the heart to seek not their own have had an enormous impact on the world. If love had not motivated women who are a part of our spiritual heritage to seek not their own, there would have been no missions as we know them today, prison reform would still be in the dark ages, nursing would be undeveloped, and orphans would still roam the streets begging for food. This is some sorority! Join the sorority of sisters whose expansive souls, through deeds of loving-kindness, have brought Christ and belonging to the most hopeless and helpless "element." Why not experience Kenya at sixty? Why not fill your house with children when you are seventy? A woman who expands her heart to God's dimensions may find life taking on a more adventurous tone as the calendar marches through her years. What old-age surprises and delights lay ahead for a woman who is a friend of God's and a friend of his friends? Anything could happen! Inner Zambia! Outer Mongolia! Who knows?

Don't be held back by the "Tsk, Tsk, Tsk" from the religiously correct, the shrunken souled, who think religion is about knowing who is "in" and who is "out." Take heart. Enlarge your soul to include all of Jesus' friends. Live like that, and your life will have made a difference. Your spiritual track record will be clear, your banner unfurled and beautiful, your lineage of spiritual children large and diverse, and your soul perfectly fit for membership in heaven, an eternally suitable companion for the heart of God.

"O God, enlarge my soul to perfectly fit the dimensions of your heart. Sensitize me to any attitude of snobbery. Help me to feel the pain of those the whole world thinks of as N.O.K. Give me a holy repulsion for anything that would exclude them from your love. Amen."

Nine

❧

A Tree Grows in Wheaton

But the godly shall flourish like palm trees, and grow tall as the cedars of Lebanon. For they are transplanted into the Lord's own garden, and are under his personal care. Even in old age they will still produce fruit and be vital and green.

—Psalm 92:12–14 (TLB)

[Love] is not easily angered, it keeps no record of wrongs.

—1 Corinthians 13:5

*H*ave you ever sustained a wound to your soul so painful it threatened to become your emotional focal point for years? Maybe you have taken in some soul damage. If so, then let me tell you about an inconspicuous tree that grows in my hometown, Wheaton, Illinois. It looks ordinary. It is not. I should know. I planted it when I was seven years old. Most people pass it by without even seeing it. If I had my way they would notice it; they would know its story. It really should have its very own bronze plaque.

Although the tree is intimately linked to my becoming, the plaque would not announce anything so mundane as, "THIS TREE WAS PLANTED BY LOCAL CITIZEN VALERIE BURTON BELL." No, no.

Even though I think it is a very sweet thing that the twig I brought home from school on Arbor Day and planted so carefully under the supervision of my father is still growing, even I have to admit such information is not exactly loaded with historical interest, local or otherwise. No, the plaque would tell my tree's real and hidden story. It would declare: "TAKE NOTE, CITIZENS AND VISITORS OF OUR FAIR CITY! THIS AMAZING TREE, AGAINST ALL ODDS, SURVIVED KATHY FOSTER."

Who was Kathy Foster? She was my best and worst first-grade friend. Normally we enjoyed each other, but when we were in the worst-of-friends mode, our relationship swung sharply to animosity. Then our passions ran to grand physical fights. I remember a few times when our relationship deteriorated to outright barbarity, with wrestling on the ground, washing of the other's face in mud, and pulling each other's pigtails until our fists were full of each other's hair. I do not exactly remember winning those contests. I usually lost. But I do credit Kathy Foster with helping me discover I had speedy feet.

But the meanest thing Kathy Foster ever did to me she did to my beloved twig tree. She did it more than once. When she could not catch me and she could not wrestle me and she could not wash my face in mud and she could not pull my hair, she turned her attention on my poor, precious, sitting duck of a sapling. Trees have many attributes, but speedy feet is not one of them!

Oh, she was covert! She came at night. Under the cover of darkness, she would sneak, implementing a plan that, come morning, would break my heart. After one of her many nocturnal visits, I would wake to discover my precious planting, broken off at its base, stripped of leaves and branches, naked and helpless, a mute and twiggy testament to her cruelty.

That tree should have died. I mourned its death many times. But amazingly, Kathy Foster never managed to actually kill that tree. She only maimed it mightily. Wherever she is (if early indications are any predictors, she is probably denuding rain forests and contributing single-handedly to global warming), I wish she could see my proud beauty today! It is tall—a majestic being two to three times the height of my former two-story home. This lovely arboreal creature, with its widespread limbs and thick trunk, raises your eyes up, up, up. Who would ever guess it had been a victim of Kathy Foster forty years ago? It looks just like other trees grown under totally favorable conditions.

Apparently it has forgotten Kathy Foster. Today it bears no visible scars. It has kept no record of wrongs. It grew past its pain. It grew past its enemy's destructive intentions for it. My seedling, abused and broken so many times, has become, to all appearances, a regular pillar of the community. For what Kathy Foster did not know—nor did I, at the time—is that the secret of a tree's strength lies beneath the ground, where you and I cannot see. The secret to survival is in the roots.

Long before a woman's middle years she learns that speedy feet are not enough to survive this sick world for very long. When it comes to those whose intentions toward us are evil— our friends who would also be our enemies—we learn that we cannot always outrun them, escape them, change their minds, or divert their evil plans for our lives. Furthermore, should we escape them on one level—when they cannot catch us, when they cannot wrestle us, when they cannot wash our face in mud, when they cannot pull out our hair—then they turn their attention to wounding what is most vulnerable: They go for our souls.

As a group, we women are intimate with abuse. We are beaten. We are emotionally abused. We are betrayed by those who profess to love us. We are sitting ducks for those who are bigger, meaner, angrier, and sicker. What woman has not on some level felt broken off at the ground, naked, and left to die? By middle age most women have experienced their own Kathy Fosters.

Surviving Our Best and Worst Friends

What is worse than experiencing the intimate pain of being wronged by a friend? A friend told me her experience of betrayal by a best and worst friend. Everything seemed to be going well between them. And so, one day without any hesitation, she welcomed a breakfast invitation from this "best friend."

The "friend" had another agenda besides breakfast, however. Midway through the meal she pulled out a stack of three-by-five cards. It was literally a record of wrongs, a list of nurtured grievances; everything that had ever given the slightest offense was recorded against my friend in black and white. The accusations were not untrue, but perhaps that was what made it all so painful. It was truth interpreted at the worst possible level.

Now, this stack of three-by-five cards contained not only her accuser's own personal record of grievances; the friend had done research. She had probed for dirt. She questioned other women in their friendship circle about their "true feelings" about this woman, dug for negative comments, initiated derogatory conversations and, without their knowledge, recorded all that had been privately confided. She had filed those deprecatory comments, which resulted primarily from her aggressive hunting expedition, on three-by-five cards as well!

When her best and worst friend was done with her record of wrongs, my friend believed she did not have a friend left in the world. She felt broken off at ground level. Only later did she learn how her other friends were manipulated into this woman's agenda—only after she had moved away from the community, specifically away from her friends, because she felt so humiliated. Is that evil or what?

We can survive our own friends, our own families, and those who should make for our best—but end up being our worst—relationships, if we understand what I did not understand in first grade: The secret to survival is in the roots. The imagery of Scripture is so clear. We are to be like trees planted by the streams of water (Psalm 1:3). Our souls are to grow deep into God. Our strength, our healing, our health, our very survival, not to mention whether we age successfully, is dependent on the depth and breadth and development of our soul in God's soil. If we have roots deep into God, others can try to break us off; they may even maim us mightily, but they will not be able to destroy us. We will be grounded in God.

Places of the Soul—What Every Woman Needs

Undoubtedly, every woman who is interested in caring for her soul needs a place to go for her spiritual development. I believe every woman would benefit from a setting that is conducive to deeper thought and internal work. Do you have a place—a porch, a chair, a certain room—to which you gravitate? If so, this might be an indication that your soul is longing to do some "rooting."

I suppose a soulful place would be different for different women. My bedroom is the most soulful room of our home. It is the place where my soul roots itself in God. We do not own a real bed, just a mattress on a frame, minus head- and footboard. Our bed sits in an alcove looking out a bank of windows that sweep three-fourths of the room. It is arbored with grapevine and layered with chintz and plaid pillows. A deeply cushioned couch and wicker chairs sit across from the bed in this bank of windows. Plants fill the empty spaces, giving the impression of the outside being inside. It feels like a bird's nest or tree house, drenched in light from skylights, open to the wind and temperature and sounds of the outdoors.

Instead of a headboard, an antique ironing board, whose aging patina I love, serves as a shelf. My taste runs to anything that is mellowed, scarred, or cracked with age—especially if it was previously used by someone I love. Nothing in this room is simply material or plastic or attainable by walking into a showroom and buying the whole kit and caboodle. Each item has a unique story, a particular history, a definite soul. And so my home has been shaped with befores and afters, thens and nows. Whatever your particular style—and it certainly does not need to be the same as mine—establish a place in your home that ministers to your spirit, that comforts you visually, physically, and spiritually.

Investing in Your Soul's Care

Lately I have been sharing my special spot with friends. It is a place that lends itself to a quiet conversation over a cup of coffee. I also want to show my friends my soul library. I think of it as a soul care station. Through the years I have invested in this soul library with time and money and thought. Just as stylish women invest in their wardrobes, and gourmands invest in their kitchens, a soulful woman will gravitate toward acquiring books, journals, and other soul tools that are investments in her soul. Hand-carved bookends from an overseas trip hold my treasures on the old, ironing board bookshelf above my bed. In the pages between those bookends, my soul's roots have spiritually rooted, fingered, filigreed, and feathered into God.

When I could not run fast enough, when I have been interpreted at the worst possible level, when the record of my wrongs has been nurtured by those I thought were my friends, when my best friends became my worst friends, here, through the years, I have found nurture and strength in God.

Journals

What are these tools that have sustained my soul in God through the years? To begin, are two types of journals. One is a leather-bound three-ring notebook filled with lined paper. It is stationary. By that I mean that I do not travel with it or take it to Bible studies or church because I would feel lost if I misplaced it and exposed if other eyes read it. That is why I also have a traveling journal. It is clothbound with bound, lined pages—the kind of empty book you can buy at any bookstore. It travels with me to my small prayer groups and lets me record prayer requests, phone numbers, and addresses of group members, or things I have learned at Bible study or at church.

My stationary journal is an eclectic collection of information, not so much a diary but a record of where my mind has been. I try to keep a journal beside me as I read. A "Peanuts" cartoon floats in the inside cover; an article I want to save might be stuck between later pages. A "to do" list might be scribbled in the margins alongside quotes from a book I am reading. But for all its apparent disarray, the journal is loosely organized into four major sections.

1. A Record of What I Read

In the first section I keep a record of everything I read. Quotes from *A Midwife's Tale: The Life of Martha Ballad Based on Her Diary 1785–1812* fill one page right next to vocabulary words culled from *From Beirut to Jerusalem*. In the course of my reading I collect words. This section contains several pages of words I enjoy and appreciate for their specificity and descriptive power. New words are a delight. I do not know when, but eventually I will use words like *prelactical* (relating to high-ranking member of clergy), *epithet* (term used to characterize someone), *euphemism* (substituting mild term for something harsh, blunt, or offensive), and *middlesence* (adolescence the second time around). Are those great words? I think so!

In addition to collecting words as I read, I keep a record of interesting thoughts or quotes that captivate me or cause me to think. These are listed under the title pages of the books I read. And while this information may not all appear "spiritual," it feeds my soul. St. Augustine said, "All truth is God's truth," and I have found that the trails of truth in art, history, science, and literature serve to highlight different facets of God. All truth enlarges me, roots me deeper into God.

2. A Record of Encouraging Words

In the second section in my journal, I record conversations with other people that have helped me spiritually. Sometimes I'll write down gems from sermons I've heard. Or maybe I'll record a snatch of an encouraging exchange with my children, husband, and my friends. This section of my journal is a record of my memorable human interactions.

For instance, one of my entries relates to an extended conversation with a trusted friend during a particularly difficult time in my life. I had shared the pain I was feeling because another close, personal friend had refused to work through the problems in our relationship. She had wounded me personally, unfairly, and deeply. Over several years, my attempts at reconciliation (stumbling though they may have been) were repeatedly brushed aside. My last serious effort to restore the relationship was essentially ignored. When I tried to tell her I was in pain over our estrangement, she responded with a terse, "I'm just too busy to deal with this now!" End of conversation. End of relationship. That was years ago. It felt like Kathy Foster all over again, except grown-up style. When I tearfully confided my hurt and frustration over this damaged relationship to my trusted friend, when I admitted that what had begun as hurt in my life had through the years begun to feel more like hate, she comforted me with these words, "God is digging a deep well of tears in your life that others can drink from and be healed." Her words ministered a fresh hope to me that out of this relationship gone bad, one I can't seem to restore, God will still do his work. I always remember when I reread this passage in my journal to trust God and not lose hope.

3. A Record of My Inner Life

My journal is the primary recorder and organizer of my soul. It reflects my inner life; it is a kind of soul mirror. It helps me articulate and put into words what were only vague feelings and impressions. *So that's what it is!* is often the feeling I have as I read what I have written. They perform a job of holding truth about my soul up to my consciousness.

The third section is a dated portion in which I take a slightly more traditional but not very literary approach to recording my thoughts and the activities of my days. Like many other people, the thought of having to be literary in my private moments is intimidating. I settle for much less on these pages. I remind myself that this is not for publication, but just for my own recording. I loosen up my expectations and thereby allow my thoughts to flow almost in a stream of consciousness. Most important, I do not allow myself to be discouraged if I miss a week or am sporadic. This journal is for me; I do not let it beat me up with self-accusations.

4. A Record of Prayer

Through the years I have filled in the pages of this fourth category with hymns and written prayers, both of my own making and from other sources, such as the *Oxford Book of Prayer* and hymnals, which I keep in my soul library and which I consider important contributors to deepening spiritually. Even when I feel I cannot pray (have you noticed the times when you need to pray are often the times when you have the least energy to think in words?), I can read through my prayer journal; in the words of a hymn or the ancient prayer of a church father or the simple prayer of an African child, I have found comfort and strength. My journal also contains several sets of completely filled-in twelve-step prayers like those I discussed in chapter four.

The One-Year Bible: A Personal Record of God's Faithfulness

Shelf space in my soul library includes other important implements for soul development, such as my copy of *The One-Year Bible*. I read through *The One-Year Bible* every year and have done this for several years. This Bible is divided into daily reading. Each day has a reading from the Old Testament, the New Testament, the Psalms, and Proverbs. I use the simplest version, *The Living Bible*, as I find it makes the Bible characters seem more like real people who might be living today. I use this particular Bible like a workbook. The pages are underlined and highlighted. Each day I read, I record the year at the top of the page by the date. Whatever stands out to me, I mark. That way

I do not lose any great spiritual gems. They are there for me to remember next year as well.

For instance, on July 18 one year I remarked "AMAZING!" next to Romans 4:20, which says, "But Abraham never doubted. He believed God, for his faith and trust grew ever stronger, and he praised God for this blessing before it happened. He was completely sure that God was well able to do anything he promised" (TLB). That was especially amazing to me at the time—particularly because my own ability to trust was running low on that particular July 18, when I read about Abraham who *never* doubted!

Additionally, I record major life events on these Bible pages: the day Brendan, our older son, was accepted at the college of his choice; the day I took skiing lessons and God showed me a spiritual lesson in the midst of my fear; the times when prayers have been directly answered. One day God gave me this verse when I was struggling with a difficult person: "Don't be impatient for the Lord to act! Keep traveling steadily along his pathway and in due season he will honor you with every blessing" (Psalm 37:34 TLB). He not only gave me the promise, but amazingly only a few dates later, "Mr. Ornery" was suddenly removed from the situation in which we had been having contact. I had been miraculously delivered! "There is a God!" is scribbled on that date. I would not be shocked if a "Hallelujah!" went out from that difficult person's side as well! He had been delivered from me!

I derive incredible strength and humor from the incidents and anecdotes I've recorded in previous years. These Bible pages are the stories of other people's spiritual journeys, but used in this way they also become my own. My scribblings and underlinings and highlightings are shorthand versions of the history of my own spiritual root growing through the years. They give witness to the journey my soul has traveled. They record how God has helped me grow past my own wounds and are a testament to God's incredible faithfulness.

Other Books as Soul Tools

Several other books, divided into daily readings, are in my spiritual library. *My Utmost For His Highest* by Oswald Chambers, *Morning and Evening* by Charles Spurgeon, *Listening to Your Life* by Frederick Buechner, *The Art of Life: A Month of Daily Devotional Readings from the Writings of Edith Schaeffer*, *Whispers of His Power: Daily Devotional Readings* by Amy Carmichael, and the classic *Streams in the Desert* by Mrs. Charles E. Cowman. I use these book as workbooks also, scribbling and highlighting passages that are particularly meaningful. I do not get to these books as faithfully as I read *The One-Year Bible*, but I do like to get to one or more of them at least a couple of days every week.

The leftover space in my bookends I use for books I am reading. Currently this space is filled with a book on Joan of Arc I picked up at a secondhand bookstore. Usually beside my bookends are a pile of books I am reading or wanting to read. This is an eclectic gathering that currently brings together *Amazing Grace: The Lives of Children and the Conscience of a Nation* by Jonathan Kozol, *Chicken Soup for the Soul: 101 Stories to Open the Heart and Rekindle the Spirit* by Jack Canfield and Mark Victor Hansen, and two biographies, *Grace,* by Robert Lacey, and *Henry Plantagenet,* by Richard Barber.

Growing Beyond Our Fascinating Wounds

Why do I mention this library of tools in detail? I want to give you a picture of the kind of material that deepens a woman's soul. There is very little material I would classify as "felt-need" material on this shelf. Felt-need reading—reading that comforts a personal need—can have an important place in a woman's life, but I am concerned that Christian women are buying and being marketed to almost exclusively on that level. I know I sound a little like an old crab on this point, and even as I say it I realize there are many exceptions to this concept, but felt-need books should be for a season, not a lifetime, just as counseling should be for a season, not a lifetime. Read only on a comfort level, and we can become stuck there and never move on.

We so easily become absorbed with our wounds. They hold an enormous fascination for most of us. But when we become absorbed with our wounds, we run the risk of becoming a self-focused generation of Christian women. I fear that. In this perpetual wounded condition, we are made null and void for the larger spiritual picture. Satan knows the larger issues of our lives can be won if Christian women become stuck, absorbed with their own areas of need. At some point we must begin to read and form our soul around things that challenge us, not just things that comfort us. So read what stretches and expands, not only what comforts and focuses on your needs.

What do you really want for your own soul development? I know what I want. I cannot be a woman without broken places, but I want to be a woman who grows beyond her broken places. I want my life to keep no record of wrongs. I do not want to experience arrested development of my soul because I am stuck nursing the grievances I have against others. If envy is the cannibal of the soul, and self is soul's slaver, then a lifestyle that keeps a record of wrongs is a lifestyle devoted continually to picking the scabs of the soul. Picking soul scabs by nurturing grievances and wounds, keeping a record of wrongs, makes a soul's scar grow larger and larger but never really heal. When we hurt in this way, the smallest things give us offense—or to use Scripture's description, we are easily angered, hypersensitive, and emotionally on edge. We are like twig trees that never grow up. Our jagged, wounded edges are exposed to the elements, but we never grow beyond them; we never experience new growth and healing.

A "Becoming" Formed to Pain

Some women's self-definition is formed by pain. In fact, if their pain would somehow miraculously dry up and blow away, some women would have little left. Sarah's mother, Andrea, was like that. Andrea's childhood had been extremely difficult, but as she became an adult, she never dealt with her pain on a spiritual level. One of the results of this unresolved childhood pain was that she was easily offended, always raw-edged, and ready to jump to the worst possible interpretation of other people. She never met a relational bridge she couldn't burn!

Sarah remembers when she was a young child that her mother had an argument with a neighbor woman. As an apology, the neighbor sent her mother a dozen long-stemmed roses. It was a kind and elegant gesture. But Andrea would not accept the apology. She left the roses, still boxed and unopened, in the driveway, within her neighbor's sight, to die. They stayed in the driveway for several weeks. She never accepted her neighbor's apology or made things right again. The dead roses became the symbolic pattern for all her relationships. One by one—husband, children, neighbors—all of her relationships died, killed by her own pattern of nurturing records of wrongs against others.

What a sad development of soul. Wounds that never heal. Bridges that are never mended. A soul broken off and stunted in growth, molded by unforgiveness.

Spiritual Healing for Broken-Off Places

How do we keep from being caught in this nongrowth pattern? How do we mend when it feels as if the same people keep breaking us off at the ground? What if my friend who was "just too busy to deal with this now" never tries to work out our relationship and she leaves me with this pain? What if we never hear "I'm sorry" from those who wound and abuse us? When our best friends become our worst friends, is the only solution to pack our bags and move out of town and hope our pain doesn't show up in the next place?

The answer is forgiveness. Spiritual healing. We need to let go of the record of wrongs against those who have hurt us. We need to stop picking our fascinating scabs. It is the only way to heal the pain. It is the only way to grow past those breaks in our lives.

But forgiveness is "the hardest trick in the whole bag of person relationships."[1] It is the most demanding soul work of all. Why? Because forgiving goes against our tendency to seek fairness and justice, to have our voice heard. When we forgive, sometimes we feel that the offender has gotten off without paying for his or her offense. Lewis B. Smedes says,

> When you suspect that forgiving is not fair, you worry that people who hurt you are not getting what is coming to them. But you worry, too, that you are getting a bad deal; you get hurt and do not get even. Forgiving may not seem fair to the one who must do the forgiving. ... But forgiving is the *only* way to be fair to yourself.
>
> Recall the pain of being wronged, the hurt of being stung, cheated, demeaned. Doesn't the memory of it fuel the fire of fury again, reheat the pain again, make it hurt again? Suppose you never forgive, suppose you feel the hurt each

time your memory lights on the people who did you wrong. And suppose you have a compulsion to think of them constantly. You have become a prisoner of your own pain; you are locked in a torture chamber of your own making.

The only way to heal the pain that will not heal itself is to forgive the person who hurt you. . . . When you release the wrongdoer of wrong, you cut a malignant tumor out of your inner life. You set a prisoner free, but you discover that the real prisoner was yourself.[2]

I am finding that forgiving is a process. I might do well at not dwelling on my wounds for a while; I may even begin to feel some mercy toward those who have wounded me. But then it starts all over again. I remember the pain, and before I know it, I'm picking my scabs, reviewing the wrongs I have against the person who wounded me. I am no longer wishing the person well, but feeling as though she should fall into one! Sometimes the work of forgiveness seems to be a forever job. I must begin the forgiveness process all over again. When I hear a soft, tempting, inner voice that reminds me of how large the offense was against me, I know I must remember who I am in God.

I am not a woman who is conformed to my pain, whose self-definition is the litany of sins that has been committed against me, who would have little left were I to lose it. No. I am a woman whose soul is forming to God. I cannot control how others treat me, but I can control my own response. I choose to relate to others based on my own character, not theirs. That is a tremendously freeing concept! My soul, formed in its "becoming" to the dimensions of God's love, can extend forgiveness, even when the other person is not worthy, never says the word "sorry," or ever shows a grain of remorse. My offender has no power over me. I hurt, but I do not become stuck there. I grow beyond the break and eventually past the power of the pain.

I do not want to become a woman like Sarah's mother, Andrea. I want, instead, to be a woman who is really tough for the bad guys to take down. I do not intend to be sidelined from the larger issues because of my own fascinating wounds. That is when I remember a woman who taught me about growing past personal pain. Her pain was extreme, but her response was "classic soul," formed to the dimensions of God's love.

A Woman's Story of Brokenness

Dr. Helen Roseveare was a single, middle-aged medical missionary to the Congo, now Zaire, during the Simba rebellion. This was the story she told about being broken off—like my tree—one horrible day in 1964.

> I could not cancel out . . . the memory of that awful night of 29 October 1964 . . . the shattering hammering at the double doors of my bungalow home in the early hours of the morning; the rough, hoarse voice demanding entry in the name of the rebel army; the fear—oh, that dreadful physical torture of fear. . . .
>
> As I nervously clutched a flimsy housecoat over my nightdress, pulling back the bolts of the door, God had seemed very far away and I had felt very, very small and alone. They had swarmed in, rough, uncouth, jeering men in various oddly-assorted garments, smelling of dirt and drink, demanding the man of the house.
>
> They searched the house; their greedy hands stole what they saw, and their greedy eyes sought me in the glare of the torches. One touched me, and I winced and drew

myself inwards. They started to go, stumbling and drunken, laughing and wicked.

The lieutenant had called me back, down the short corridor to my bedroom. "Go in and . . ." Perhaps I didn't hear: perhaps the hammering in my ears of surging blood and fear made me *think* he said "undress": he denied it later. I fled out into the dark night, stumbling in the mud, fighting down wild panic as I fell.

"My God, where are You now? Where is Your peace now? Where victory?"

The soldiers came. Naked beams of light stabbed the night, and I was alone. They found me, dragged me to my feet, struck me over the head and shoulders, flung me to the ground, kicked me, dragged me to my feet only to strike me again—the sickening, searing pain of a broken tooth, a mouth full of sticky blood, my glasses gone. Beyond sense, numb with horror and unknown fear, driven, dragged, pushed back to my own house—yelled at, insulted, cursed.

"My God, my God, why have You forgotten me, forsaken me?"—the wild cry of a tortured heart—alone, oh, how alone!

Suddenly Christ was there. No vision, no voice, but His very real presence. . . . Then as swiftly He spoke to my heart: "They're not fighting you: these blows, all this wickedness, is against Me. All I ask is the loan of your body. Will you share with Me one hour in My sufferings for these who need My love?"[3]

Dr. Roseveare paraphrased her words from Christ that night this way, "Helen, it's only body."

She had come to this country to love its people, but some had returned her love with hatred. She could not outrun them, escape them, change their minds, or divert their evil plans for her life. And when they were done wrestling her, washing her face in mud, and pulling out her hair, they thought they had destroyed her. They thought it was the end of her, of her sanity, her health, and her ministry. But they did not understand what many do not understand. The secret to survival is in the roots.

She was mightily maimed, but because she had roots, she did not need to keep a record of wrongs. She was not destroyed; in fact, she was stronger for having suffered them. Her ministry was deeper, and she returned to that country after the war was over. Her strong message is still heard because she grew past the pain, and amazingly, from that exact wounded place in her life great ministry has grown: Her message of survival, of God's grace in the midst of feminine destruction, rape, torture, fear, sounds strong to women today. *They could only have her body. They could never have her soul!* Her soul was under God's own personal care.

When Kathy Foster Goes for Your Soul

What evil agenda have you encountered? Is Kathy Foster going for your soul? When you have been interpreted in the lowest possible way, when those who should have been your best friends become your worst, when speedy feet are not enough to escape them, remember my tree. Consider there may be a greater issue at stake: What wound has the Evil One hoped to give your God by breaking you in two? How has he hoped to negate your spiritual effectiveness?

Care for your soul, attend to the spiritual issues, and then watch how God fights the plans of the Evil One that have come against you to destroy your soul and wound your God. At that very place where you have been broken off and left to die, a sprout will grow, and another until you become tall, a soul that is a place of shelter and shade for all who pass by. And by so growing, you will lift the eyes of the world up, up, up to your God.

Then even in old age you will produce fruit and be vital and green. You will have foiled the destructive plans of evil for your life. Then those who know your story will be amazed and realize you are not what you appear to be—just ordinary—but rather, you are very special indeed.

Grow despite the Kathy Fosters of your world. They thought you were so easy to break off. They are looking down for a stunted, deformed, little twig tree. Freak them out. Point their eyes up, up, up. Grow to be flourishing and tall. Stand firm. Bear fruit. Forgive. Remember, they do not know what you know. The secret to survival is in your roots. The forgiving soul belongs to God alone. Grow beyond the wound. Feel the pain lessen. Form your soul to God's loving dimensions. And who knows, when you are old and there are many rings on your life tree, maybe someone will tell your story. Someone really should note your amazing survival with a plaque. I can see it by your front door now: "TAKE NOTE, CITIZENS AND VISITORS OF OUR FAIR CITY! THIS AMAZING WOMAN, AGAINST ALL ODDS, SURVIVED KATHY FOSTER. EVEN IN HER OLD AGE SHE IS LIKE A TREE TRANSPLANTED INTO GOD'S OWN GARDEN. SHE IS UNDER HIS PERSONAL CARE."

Ten

"Younging"

An aged man is but a paltry thing,
A tattered coat upon a stick, unless
Soul clap its hands and sing.

—William Butler Yeats, *Sailing to Byzantium*

Love does not delight in evil but rejoices with the truth.

—1 Corinthians 13:6

Some time ago I took an aging awareness test. I learned a lot. It is amazing what I did not know about growing older. The test revealed some of my preconceived prejudices, the lies I have believed about what it is like to be old.

A true-false question stated, "Senility or senile dementia is a normal part of body breakdown in the aging process." I answered true. I was wrong. It was explained that senility is no more normal for old age than is heart disease or cancer. Hmm... interesting.

In fact, most of the things I learned that day were good news. Another true-false question I missed: "After the age of sixty-five, the ability to learn is greatly diminished." I said true. Wrong again. I also learned that creativity does not diminish with age, that most older people are not weak and in poor health, and that only five percent of elderly people need nursing care.

While it is true that over half of those older than sixty-five experience vision loss or vision change and a third suffer some kind of hearing loss, some things are gained. The losses are balanced by positives such as the increase in activity of people after retirement. That explains why seniors contribute to society the highest voting and volunteer rates. I learned that interest in sexual activity continues and that sexual capabilities do not rapidly diminish after sixty-five. It was reassuring to know that most aging people do not become bag ladies in their later years; in fact, only fifteen percent have severe economic problems, with ten percent living below the poverty level.

Images Matter

How could I have been so far off? Maybe it is because when I think of aging, certain images fill my mind. In our culture old women are often characterized as poor or physically handicapped or ditzy. Often they are portrayed as a joke. I think of several TV commercials: "Where's the beef?" was a question that successfully sold hamburgers by poking a too-close camera at an up-front, in-your-face, crusty, old woman. "I've fallen and I can't get up!" rings in our ears as a warning of living later life with all the charm and body movement of a sack of potatoes. And as for senility, we can thank a certain restaurant for giving us the adorable but ditzy Lenny—oops!—Denny sisters.

Now, I can see the humor in those commercials, but there is a problem here: They are not benign. These eccentric and negative images of aging are so memorable they really stick. They have staying power. Further ingraining our negative stereotypes about older women, these unforgettable images are rarely balanced by ones that speak the positive truths about aging women in equally memorable ways. Although I know many older women who are still attractive, gorgeous even, whose minds are sharp and social skills charming, mostly as a culture we think of such older women as the exception. Our collective thinking about aging women is overwhelmingly negative.

There is a subtle power in these images—because what we believe about aging has an enormous influence. We start to believe these negative images are universal and inevitable. What we believe about the aging process is what we may actually become.

How Wilma "Younged"

I enjoy watching the movies of our family from my own childhood. But it never ceases to amaze me how much older my mother, Wilma, looked when we were children than how she looked when she was actually older. Her childhood had been difficult. Her father was an alcoholic, and her mother struggled to provide for her children. My mother dragged a lot of sadness into her adult life.

But when I see pictures taken later of my mother, something strikes me. Her later years were much better than her early ones. She lost weight; she colored her gray hair; she traveled; she was a social butterfly; she learned the magic of makeup; and although she had never had the opportunity to go to college, she self-educated. She laughed more. She enjoyed more. She became accomplished. (She received an honorary doctorate for her poetry.) She dressed better. The pictures of her taken in her sixties are so much more attractive than the dowdy ones of her taken in her early forties. She definitely "younged." I know no other way to describe her process of advancing through the years.

Let me explain that no fountain of youth or secret herbal potion can be credited with my mother's change. She did not undergo a face-lift. She had never heard of an antioxidant. Her "younging" was a job performed totally and completely by her spirit. It was exclusively an interior job. Her soul seemed to rid itself of a lot of baggage along the way. She traveled those last years of her life with a blitheness of spirit that amazed and sometimes worried us. She broke her leg riding a bicycle. After my father died, she fell madly and passionately into the kind of love you would expect from a much younger woman. She reveled in attending lectures and learning new things. She gathered strawberries and wildflowers and new friends. Through her eyes I saw her friends as all near-genius writers and artists and thinkers. Because she loved them, she enlarged them and endowed them with amazing attributes.

I thought she had become a little dangerous. She was certainly eyebrow-raising! I worried that she had gone over some edge of her soul and had lost sight of her previous appropriate boundaries. When I expressed embarrassment to a friend about her public displays of affection with her new fiancé, I had to be reminded, "Valerie, just be glad she can feel these things at her age."

I was young, proper, and conventional. I was already poised for my Protestant nun stage when I would crepe my soul in browns, blacks, and navy blues. My mother, in contrast, was much younger than I. She was done with the dumpy, frumpy, dowdy, weighted-down forties approach to life; she had been there, done that. She was almost seventy, and her soul blazed with hot pinks and lemon yellows. This was not the wearing of purple and red just for the shock value. Her clothing appropriately reflected her joy, not her lack of social propriety. It was as if she had thrown out every youthful weight she had carried in her early years and was now squeezing all the joy she could from life. Every drop.

Victor Hugo said, "When grace is joined with wrinkles it is adorable." Adorable or not, I still worried about her. I worried if she would be able to handle physically her own hyperactive, live-to-the-max lifestyle. Her angina was so severe that I usually had to carry not only my own purse, diaper bag, et cetera, but her purse as well. And then what I feared happened. She suffered a massive heart attack at sixty-nine. I really think the joy factor was too much for her heart. The last pictures taken of her were of her laughing with tears running down her cheeks. I remember the evening so clearly. We had laughed so hard my jaws hurt the next day.

Then, suddenly, she died. She died dancing. Square dancing. She had just turned to her friends and said, "Oh, what fun!" Then she slumped over in her chair and bang! . . . she was gone.

Endings Better Than Our Beginnings

Life was better at the end than it was at the beginning for my mother. I admire that. I think that I, too, would like to die dancing. Why not throw off the weights of early living and travel lighter as I age? I want to dress my soul more brightly — to rid myself of the dark, depressed, mourning clothes of my youth and wrap myself instead in the colors of fireworks. (I hope my children will not be too shocked!) When will I pick strawberries and wildflowers and endow my friends with so much love that they become people of high value to all who know them through me — when, if not now? Here's to many "mornings after" when my jaw hurts from laughing so hard the night before! Maybe I will manage to raise a few stodgy eyebrows and be thought of as somewhat dangerous. That would be great! Oh, that my ending would be better than my beginning! I intend to get better at this thing called living.

Don't you?

Here is the thing: the art of living comes before the art of dying. We cannot die dancing if we do not live dancing. We cannot die laughing if we do not live laughing. We cannot die clapping and toe tapping and bouncing babies and singing if we do not learn how to live that way.

It is not enough to plaster on a smile and polish the exterior cup. No plastic surgeon can perform this magic. No, "younging" is strictly an interior job. Love of life flows from the soul, not the body. You cannot fake "younging." It must come from the deep interior self that knows the truth about aging and rejoices.

They tell us lies, you know. They tell us it is inappropriate to have old feet that are also dancing feet. They intimate that falling in love when we are older is unseemly, an embarrassment to our children. We are told that only young women are beautiful. When we have the most life experience, we are often made to think that we have the least to offer. Is that a perverse plan or what? "Slow down!" we are told. "Try not to worry others. Take up cross-stitching! Settle down!" They encourage us to stay at home; after all, what would happen if we should experience a heart attack while visiting Africa? "Do you really want to die on safari, away from a modern, sterile hospital, having so much fun it kills you?"

What are these messages really saying? They are telling us that life is over even before our hearts stop pounding and our lungs stop breathing. It is a lie. It is a lie, though sometimes well intended, that can kill our spirits. It is a lie that is laid often and unworthily at the life of older women.

All I can say is, watch out, my sons, Brendan and Justin! I hope you are ready for the days to come. I am already laughing at them in anticipation, knowing, because I raised you, that you deserve anything I might dish out in old age. Remember the little incident when your father and I were out of the country and you hauled the mattresses out of the house and used them as cushions when you jumped, flipped, and swan-dived off the roof? Remember the time you dyed your hair orange just before our relatives visited from California? Remember when you gave that little girl in first grade a bloody nose . . . or your freshman year in college when you posed for your picture without a shirt and wearing a huge Afro-wig, which will remain in your college yearbook for generations to come?! Try not to forget how graciously I handled those incidents when you are dealing with the eccentricities of my growing older! I do not intend to die until I stop breathing. Be warned. I have many good laughs ahead of me.

Rejoice in the Truth About Aging

What do you want to believe? Lies that will take your enjoyment of life from you prematurely? Or would you like to rejoice in truth about feminine aging? Would you like to live laughing at the days to come, dancing to the rhythms of exciting unknown tomorrows, anticipating an adventure at the next life turn? It takes discernment to ascertain the truth about growing old from cultural fiction. It takes wisdom to weed out messages of premature death and build your aging around truth that enhances life. "Love does not delight in evil but rejoices in the truth." This verse, interpreted through the growing-older grid, speaks of the ability to discern between the lies—the attitudes that wound and prematurely kill the feminine soul—and the truth that encourages us to live fully. It says to me, love your life whatever your age. Rejoice and embrace the truth. You are well and still breathing!

A Woman Who Improved with Age

In later years the ability to discern can come together as it never did in youth. Remember Sarah? She was a woman who improved with age. She was married to Abraham, the man who *never* doubted God. She is remembered mostly for two distinctive characteristics from her youth: her beauty and her barrenness. Both areas brought about low points in her life journey. Early in life she learned that beauty has its downside. Being desirous can be dangerous. She attracted the attention of the wrong kind of men—powerful men, ambitious men with driving needs to possess beautiful women. She was so turn-the-head beautiful that even the Pharaoh of Egypt noticed and wanted her. Abraham, fearing for his own life, knowing how easy it would be for a powerful man like Pharaoh to dispose of such a small technicality as a husband, asked Sarah to pose not as his wife but as his sister. She cooperated.

She was taken to live in Pharaoh's palace. In time, however, Pharaoh found out the truth and angrily returned her to Abraham. At this point in the story, Scripture is frustratingly silent. Only the discussion between Abraham and Pharaoh is recorded. It never reports Sarah's feelings or thoughts or words during this incident. We can only imagine the marital discussions that must have followed. Could she have felt anything but betrayed? It is not hard to imagine that Sarah may have welcomed the coming of a few wrinkles and the passing of youth and beauty that so strongly attracted the opposite sex. Time would mercifully resolve that issue in her life.

But time could only exasperate her barrenness. Infertility would continue to complicate her life. It would set the stage for the most ugly and selfish incident we know about her. In the light of the ticking, or silence, of her own biological clock, she wearied of waiting for God to fulfill his promise of family to Abraham. At seventy-six years of age she became extremely pragmatic (in the face of the bald realities of barrenness) and implemented a human plan. As was allowed by custom, she gave her maidservant, Hagar, to her husband to create for herself and her husband a child. When the woman became pregnant, however, Sarah became jealous. That, combined with the servant woman's disdain for Sarah's infertility, became a great irritation to Sarah. Her unguarded soul propelled her toward an evil choice. She drove pregnant Hagar into the wilderness where, apart from God's intervention, Hagar and her unborn son would certainly have died.

That is Sarah as portrayed by Scripture. She is a woman with a beautiful, polished, exterior cup, but the inside of her cup is full of bitterness, envy, anger, and unbelief. A great gap exists between her appearance and her character. Her soul is untended, ugly even.

The next time we see her is thirteen years later. It has been thirteen years of watching Hagar's son grow, thirteen years of a husband who never doubted in the face of bald realities, thirteen years more of infertility and bodily decline. But when we see her this time, she is a changed woman. She is laughing. Okay . . . it is somewhat of a naughty laugh. It is edged in cynicism. She is laughing at the renewed promise of God that Abraham would bear a son through her and that she would be the mother of nations; kings of people would come from her. Can anyone blame this almost ninety-year-old woman for laughing at this news?

But from that incredible moment on, she probably never stopped laughing. She did not have to try too hard to laugh at the days to come. It is not hard to picture her laughing with joy when she found she was actually pregnant. She probably laughed at the thought of her wrinkled, drooping breasts nursing a baby. She had to laugh when her friends speculated that her swelling belly meant she was gaining weight, and she was able to inform them she was carrying a child. Anyone would laugh watching her friends nearly drop dead at such news! She had that joy. She laughed when she felt the baby move. When she experienced her greatest life longing, when she watched her body bring forth a child, she must have been overjoyed. She must have laughed so hard her jaw ached and her wrinkled furrows filled with tears.

God even seems to catch the changed spirit of this woman. He tells Abraham to name their son Isaac, which in Hebrew means *laughter*. What else could a child of such a mother be named? Sarah's laughter blessed the world, and everyone laughed when they heard of her marvelous old-age surprise.

Can you see the difference in the before-and-after picture of Sarah? She is more beautiful in her advanced age than she was in her youth. In her earlier years, she had a beautiful body, but she also was a woman who doubted God, who schemingly took things into her own hands, and who was capable of great evil. In her old age, she experienced a metamorphosis. In her old age, she had wrinkles and bags and gray hair. But she also had a soul that laughed. The laughter was not plastered on or the result of polishing an exterior cup but the result of a change in her soul. The old Sarah was gone. A new, older but better Sarah had emerged—a woman who probably never doubted God again. God's old-age surprise of *laughter* mellowed Sarah.

She "younged" and became full of awe and wonder at God's plans. She finished better than when she began.

A Word of Advice from the Oldest Living Person

On October 17, 1995, newspapers around the world ran articles complete with pictures of the oldest living person recorded by the *Guinness Book of World Records*. A snowy-haired, deeply wrinkled, toothless face looked with blind eyes out from the page. Her name is Jeanne Calment and on October 17, 1995, she was 120 years and 238 days old—old enough to be recognized as the oldest known person who ever lived in modern times. According to the newspaper, "Calment, who celebrated the record at her old people's home in Arles in Provence in southern France, is blind, almost deaf and confined to a wheelchair but retains a reputation as a mischievous joker.

"'Always keep your smile. That's how I explain my long life. I think I will die laughing. I've only had one wrinkle and I am sitting on it,' she says with a smirk. 'Everything interests me. . . . I've had a fine life.'"[1]

She is beautiful, don't you see? She is a soul sister to Wilma and Sarah and all the other women we know who have "younged" as they advanced through the years. As the oldest living person, she's still laughing at the days to come. Her soul is draped in bright purples and daffodil yellow. Her laugh is naughty. Her smile is disarming, toothless. She probably winks at young boys and tells them that if she were ten years younger . . . ! She is a little dangerous. She blows their minds. She's earned her place in the history books. You get the feeling she might still do Africa if it were wheelchair accessible. She is over 120 years and 238 days young.

"Younging!" Yes, that is the idea! May we end better than we began. May our souls be open to surprises that mellow us toward God. May our befores and afters show us to be women who learned to trust God more. May you and I live all the days allotted to us in our lifetimes to the maximum. May we rejoice in the truth about aging: old is beautiful when the soul "youngs," claps its hands, lifts its deepest self to God, does a jig, and laughs until its jaw aches at the days full of surprises to come.

Eleven

Changes and Becomings

In the hundreds of interviews I have done with men and women in middle life, I have discovered that people are beginning to see there is the exciting potential of a new life to live: one in which they can concentrate on becoming better, stronger, deeper, wiser, funnier, freer, sexier and more attentive to living the privileged moment—even as they are getting older, lumpier, bumpier, slower and closer to the end. Instead of being a dreary tale of decline, our middle life is a progress story, a series of little victories over little deaths. It's a potential that offers exhilarating new possibilities. But only for those who are aware and prepare.

—Gail Sheehy,
New Passages: Mapping Your Life Across Time

[Love] always protects, always trusts,
always hopes, always perseveres.

—1 Corinthians 13:7

*I*n my late twenties and early thirties I traveled as a singer to women's conferences and church retreats. Singing was my identity: that is, until an enormous shift happened in my life. In one seemingly out-of-control weekend, my life redefined in mid-stream. That was the weekend when a remarkable woman showed me that when life gets tough, it is best to bend.

I was invited to an out-of-state women's conference to do the music for the weekend. The weekend started normally enough. I arrived Friday afternoon and my concert was not until Saturday night. I would have as much time as I needed on Saturday to rehearse with my accompanist. My sense of well-being would not last for long, however.

Just as I was thinking I could kick my shoes off and relax a little, around six o'clock, about an hour before the first scheduled meeting, I heard a knock on my hotel-room door. I opened it and looked out at a group of worried faces. It was the women's retreat committee. The national speaker's flight had been canceled. She would not make it on time for the evening session. They asked, "Would you be able to do your concert tonight instead of tomorrow?"

Did I have a choice? Panic set in. One hour was not enough time to pull a concert together! I rushed to the meeting room to try to squeeze in some intense practice time with my assigned accompanist—or I should say accompanists? That is when I knew it was going to be more than just an unusual weekend. Three hands accompanied me at the piano that night. Before the concert I never even had time to ask why *two* women were sitting on the piano bench playing for me. Bang! In no time the meeting room had filled, and the concert was in progress.

We tried to do our best under the circumstances, but we had to lower our standards of artistry to the basest of expectations: get through it—survive. I think we really stunned them. Yes, we definitely had our moments of humiliation. I was so rattled I forgot some of the words to my most familiar songs. My accompanists got lost at key transitional places. Our struggle was obvious to all who attended. Embarrassing!

Afterward, we fled the hotel, seeking refuge in a restaurant where no one would recognize us, where we could debrief. We were punchy with relief. There was nothing to do but laugh; laugh at ourselves, laugh at our circumstances, laugh at our mistakes. We even laughed right through the story about why three hands accompanied me that night. We should have cried, but it was a night to laugh.

A Bender, a Shifter, a Redefined Becomer

And there, in the midst of our laughter, I discovered more about the amazing woman who had been half of my accompanist team. These two musicians were in their mid-thirties. One of the women played with only one hand. She had been an accomplished pianist, but now she could no longer play the piano with two hands, having lost the movement of her left arm through a series of surgeries and other treatments for metastasized breast cancer. At the last minute her friend, the two-handed pianist, had dragged her along into this emergency scenario. Her role was to help her friend stay in the right place musically. As I look back, I think she was a "plant," someone strategically placed by God in my life, someone meant to teach me a few things, although probably neither of us realized it at the time.

She told her story lightly, delightfully aware of the irony and awkwardness of the situation our combined circumstances had brought about during this crazy night. She made us laugh about the way life sometimes spins out of control with three-handed concerts and metastasized cancer. She was so charming! It was amazing she could still laugh at anything. I was so touched by her, and although she didn't say, it occurred to me that she may have been dying. Her naughty humor and joy in less-than-perfect circumstances spoke clearly to me: You are not dead until you can no longer enjoy living.

The most potent lesson she taught me, though, she taught me the following day. The national speaker had finally arrived, but before she spoke, this same one-handed pianist played a trumpet solo. She had learned how to play only within the last year, but she played so beautifully you easily could have thought that she had played most of her life. This was one musically talented woman! Afterward, she told her story. After she lost her arm movement, when she realized she had lost the ability to play the piano (except in three-handed situations, which are fortunately rare), she told the Lord she would still like to use her musical gifts. Wasn't there an instrument she could play with only one arm?

That was how she became a trumpeter.

She was also a powerful model of how to manage heartbreaking loss. This woman was no wimp! Life had hit her hard, but she had managed to shift, to bend, to use productively what was left. What a success story! In midlife she had to shift her entire identity, but by doing so, she had also learned a secret to successful living. Bend. Shift. Redefine. Become.

Apply the Lessons Learned About Bending

Late that Saturday night, while my shoes were off and my feet were up and I was exhaling sighs of relief, another knock sounded on my door. I opened it to find the same retreat committee, the same worried faces. The national speaker had been called home to an emergency. She was unable to stay for the last meeting on Sunday morning. They asked, "Would you be willing to speak to the women?"

Did I have a choice? Panic again. They sent the national speaker off to the airport in a chartered limousine with kisses, hugs, and prayers, expressing their corporate concern for the crisis in her life. Meanwhile, I was hard at work because I had nothing prepared. I had never spoken for a group this large before. This was new and frightening. I stayed up most of that night, trying to construct a spiritual message, while a strong unspiritual urge to wring the neck of a certain national speaker kept coming to my mind.

The next morning when I stood up to speak, I looked out on over one thousand disappointed feminine faces. I was not the famous national speaker they had come to hear! Their body language spoke loudly and clearly. They whispered to each other; they shook their heads; they were not happy. I do not remember what I said. They probably do not remember what I said either. I was back to settling for the basest of expectations: Get through it—survive.

Afterward, the retreat committee was nowhere to be found. They were suffering group posttraumatic stress in one of their hotel rooms, no doubt. I realized they had forgotten about getting me to the airport. There would be no limousine send-off with hugs and kisses and thank-yous for me! Great! Now I was going to miss my flight home! Wouldn't that be the frosting on the cake to finish off the weekend! More panic!

I forgot my pride, and grabbed a woman who had been at the conference and asked if she could please drive me to the airport. She graciously agreed to help me. We streaked through the streets, a deserving target for any police officer who wanted to ticket someone that morning. Fortunately, we were not stopped. We scrambled into the terminal at the last second, both of us running through the airport, carrying my suitcases because there had been no time to check them in. One quick thank-you, one thank-you back, a mutual good-bye, and I was on the plane.

I had one last indignity to suffer, though. As I entered the plane, the steward informed me, his voice dripping with haughty superiority, that I should have checked in my bags. *Oh, duh, really?* The urge to wring certain necks seemed to be a recurring emotional theme of that weekend.

Ignoring his fussing, I found a place for my luggage (without his help), and collapsed, traumatized, into my seat. My body was quivering, my nerves totally shot; I could barely fasten my seat belt. "Oh, God! What a disaster this weekend was!" I prayed shakily, "What was that all about?"

I was not really expecting an answer to that question. I thought it was rhetorical. And then *she* came to mind, the bender, the shifter, the redefined one, the becomer, the pianist turned trumpeter. A conviction was welling up inside of me: It was no mistake that I had met that young woman this particular weekend. The image of her laughing through the cancer, playing the piano with one hand, and then blowing into her trumpet was a strong visualization I could not easily forget. She stuck with me. She was the strongest impression out of a weekend that had put my whole being into sensorial overdrive.

Even before the flight landed in Chicago, I began to think differently about my life. I realized that although the weekend had been traumatic, something inside of me had risen to the occasion. I was not intimidated by the speaking, even under those circumstances. I was comfortable. If I had been given adequate advanced warning, if I had been given normal preparation time, it occurred to me that most of the panic would not have been present at all. In fact, the nervous tension I often struggled with in singing was absent when I spoke. Was God trying to tell me something? What did all this mean?

I prayed, "Lord, I do not know what all of this means. I will let you decide. I will simply go through any doors you open for me in the future."

That was twelve years ago. It was the beginning of an entire identity change. Now invitations and opened doors are not about singing; they are about speaking. That one weekend started a change in who I would become. All I knew at the time was that the singing opportunities seemed to be drying up. I thought I was experiencing the death of my dream. I felt lost. I did not realize that I was in a transition. Before I could see that God had a plan in all of this, I wondered why God was "benching" me. Wasn't I good enough? It felt like a terrible loss, a personal small death. I had a sense, somehow, that my life had taken a lesser turn.

But God knew exactly what he was doing, even if I didn't understand it at the time. Sometimes we find by losing. To find my adult ministry gifts, I would have to let go of the child who was mother's singing daughter. I would need to learn how to bend and shift to find my redefined self.

That is how I became a speaker.

So Resistant to Change We Become Stuck

Change can come upon us suddenly. One cancer diagnosis turned a young woman from a piano player to a trumpeter. One out-of-control weekend would make another thirty-something woman look more closely at her becoming.

One moment or one sentence might change a woman's life so drastically that after it is spoken, she is no longer wife, but a widow; no longer a wife, but divorcée. One circumstance, one seemingly chance encounter, one word may bring about a change so drastic that it totally redefines a woman's life.

Very often the painful change eventually works into the positive becoming.

Menopause—much heralded as "The Change"—is just one of the changes a woman must manage during a lifetime. What "The Change" has in common with other changes of life is the sense of loss that is involved. Grief clings to what is old, what is familiar. We resist new definitions of self. We resist embracing change; we ignore its possibilities. We all cling to the stage of life that was halcyon for us.

Yet bending, shifting, redefining, and becoming are important skills to learn if we want to age successfully. Getting stuck in any particular stage of life can lead to frustration and inappropriate feminine aging.

Take professional cheerleaders, for example. I should be jealous of those gorgeous, young bodies, but actually I am always just a little embarrassed for these grown-up women. It is as if they are stuck in high school. Cheerleading was probably their high-water mark in life. While it is understandable why they might want to prolong such a perk-filled life stage, I wonder, *What is to become of such women if they do not move on?* Will we see senior citizen cheerleaders if these women continue to identify primarily with an early, well-loved stage of their lives?

Heartbreaking Loss

My heart hurts with those who are at a bending, changing, heartbreaking juncture of life. Will they survive their loss? I spoke with a friend who has been diagnosed with a rare form of sinus cancer. She has always been a beautiful woman. The future treatments may be disfiguring—the loss of an eye, the loss of a nose. As we spoke, she said, "Valerie, I hope this doesn't seem vain, but I kind of want to keep my nose." Vain? Hardly! Heartbreaking, definitely.

How can a woman survive such a devastating loss? Can she shift her identity from beautiful to disfigured and not be crushed from the heartbreak of such a loss?

Close to my heart is a family whose oldest child suffers from severe depression. He has been an honor roll student all his life. His future and potential always seemed so bright. Now, in his late teens, his life has taken a deep swing away from the happy child we once knew. His depression and accompanying desire to commit suicide has been unrelieved by medication or electric shock treatments or counseling. His parents cannot leave him alone, for fear he may take his life. Those are the good days.

The bad days are when his urge for suicide becomes over-whelmingly attractive. Then they keep him alive by commit-ting him to psychiatric hospitals, safe places where he cannot harm himself. A year that should have included the prom and graduation instead was marked by institutional commitments, suicide attempts, another round of medications. It appears that instead of college, career, and a normal existence, he may spend his life in this pattern. Their dreams of potentiality are being shattered by the possibility of their son becoming a lifetime mental patient.

Oh, God! How will they survive such a change in plans and dreams? Will they be able to deal with the shift from being par-ents of promise to parents of dementia, if need be, without being crushed under such a loss? Can even the love of a parent for a child bear this?

A Lesson from the Dolphins

A while back, I watched a fascinating nature special on TV that gave me some perspective on handling painful changes. It was about sick dolphins. The dolphins were free, but they were dying. They could be saved if they could be treated with antibiotics, but it is not easy to convince a dolphin to submit to medical treatment. They had to be caught in huge nets, snatched up from the ocean, and then pulled overboard into waiting boats.

It must have been terrifying for them. Human hands were all over them. Human voices were shouting directions. Everything must have seemed out of control. They had no way of knowing that these new experiences were well-intentioned. They had only dolphin perspective. They were at Point A. Their very survival depended on them getting to Point C. But first they had to go through Point B—an insecure place full of unknowns, a place that seemed out of control, a place where endurance seemed impossible. The whole process was necessary for them to survive and become healthy.

Marine scientists knew the stress could be too much for already-ill animals. "I hope they survive this," one said.

Life is difficult with limited perspective. Point Bs are small deaths. Personal losses. Changes that involve "lesser" definitions of self than we had hoped for. At Point B our human perspective cannot anticipate the good possibilities of Point C. God's perspective sees the whole picture. He knows that to survive spiritually, we must experience transitional periods; we must go through Point B to get to Point C. Like the marine scientists, who cared for the well-being of the dolphins, God has our best interests in mind through the whole painful process of change.

Who Are You?

Sheila Walsh, in her book, *Honestly*, describes a personal loss, a painful redefinition of self at a Point B in her life. To all appearances, Sheila was doing well. She was a successful Christian musician and the co-host of television's "700 Club." But all was not as well as it appeared. As she explained it:

> By the spring of that eventful year [1992], I knew I was losing hold. . . . I felt as if I were slowly losing my mind. Although I was still functioning on the show, I knew my distress was beginning to show. . . . I would wake up at three o'clock every morning, wide awake and afraid. Some nights I felt as if I couldn't breathe, and I would lie on my bedroom floor wishing God would take me home. "Lord, hold me," I begged. "I'm falling fast."

> It became clear to me that I could not continue as I was. I was worsening every day. . . . After talking with a doctor on the phone for a little while, he told me he believed I needed to be hospitalized. I knew the doctor was right; I knew I was beyond self-help.

> Over and over in my mind I replayed words I'd heard in the last month.

> "You might never be special again."

Later in the hospital she remembers thinking:

> How is it possible that this morning I was on national television, beautifully dressed, part of a respected Christian ministry, and now I am locked up in a psychiatric ward, not even trusted with a hair dryer?

> I had my first appointment with the doctor who would be working with me.

> He asked me a question that seemed strange to me: "Who are you?"

> I told him I was the co-host of "The 700 Club," that I was a singer, a writer, and that I knew I was floundering.

My mind went over countless photo shoots and page after page of biographical information, but I knew that this was not what he was looking for. He meant the stuff of life, the fabric of my being, but my life was what I *did*, and I didn't know what else to say.

"I don't know," I said, as tears poured down my face.

"I know that, and that is why you are here."

Like Sheila, many of us define ourselves by what we do or by our relationships (daughter of..., wife of..., mother of...). How we answer that important life question, "Who are you?" is key to aging well in the midst of inevitable loss. When we identify ourselves primarily by some life role, we will feel lost when, at some Point B, life forces us to let go. That is human perspective.

God looks at us from a different perspective. He does not define us by our roles or by our relationships. He knows us by our hearts, our character, our intrinsic eternal selves. Our souls are what identify us to God.

We look to our labels; God looks to our core. Labels like child of..., mother of..., wife of..., Christian broadcaster, author, singer, beautiful woman, teacher, businesswoman, or psychiatric patient, only describe where we have been—not who we are! Sheila will always be special. That is God's perspective. She can never lose her intrinsic worth, only her perceived worth.

We can lose many identities in life, but in the end, our souls remain. At Point C we discover that after the loss and fear, we are still here. We are so much more than our labels. We are more than our health; we are more than our beauty or our life's achievements. We are more than any defining relationship or our mental health. We are more than our image or what we are perceived to be. We can lose every drop of perceived specialness and still, soul—that deep, intrinsic, individual identifying specialness—remains.

God remains as well. Nothing can change that. A shift to internal values away from external perceptions is sustaining. A woman who cares more for her soul than she does about the labels she has acquired, who is focused on the work of becoming God's friend, has an abiding, immutable center. The perception of the cup may shift; the interior woman abides. A friend of God need have only one dread. "We regard falling from God's friendship as the only thing dreadful and we consider becoming God's friend as the only thing worthy of honor and desire."[2]

Older women have a great advantage when it comes to perceptions in life: We have experience. There have been so many Point Bs in our lives. During my father's years of mindlessness, after my mother's death, when I stopped being primarily a singer, when I was diagnosed with cancer, I learned that Point Bs, though they hurt terribly, are survivable. In my forties, I have a resource I did not have when I was younger. I have a track record with God. Throughout my life, I can say that God has been incredibly faithful and good to me. I know that some Point Bs are necessary. Without them, I would never have learned what it means to hope, what it means never to give up, what it means to trust. So much of our anxiety about the days to come fades when we look at our life through God's eternal perspective. That is why God reassures our troubled soul with the invitation to trust him—to have confidence about his good intentions for our life.

Get through the Point Bs, the changing times, the shifting times, the times of redefinition, the times when from a human perspective everything seems out of control. Do not even try to interpret what is happening. Be kind to yourself. Take a day at a time. Lower your usual high (sometimes unrealistic!) expectations; hang on; survive long enough to get to Point C.

Love Survives

Scripture says that "love always protects, always trusts, always hopes, always perseveres." I am fond of the poetic language of the King James translation of these particular verses: "[Love] beareth all things, believeth all things, hopeth all things, endureth all things."

In other words, love survives all things. It never gives up. Love casts a hopeful eye to the future and trusts that Point C will come. Love shifts away from polishing the cup of perceived worth to valuing the resources and richness of the deeper, intrinsic self. Love believes that endings can also be beginnings, that painful changes can also be positive becomings. Love bends away from heartbreak and blows into the trumpet of the days to come with one-armed hope.

A Mystery in Small Deaths

From a human perspective, there is mystery here, just as I suspect the dolphins experienced dolphin-wonder concerning the frightening events that led to their healing. When Frederick Buechner wrote about death as our greatest life loss, he also wrote truth about all the smaller deaths we experience in life:

> We find by losing. We hold fast by letting go. We become something new by ceasing to be something old. This seems to be close to the heart of that mystery. I know no more now than I ever did about the far side of death as the last letting-go of all, but I begin to know that I do not need to know and that I do not need to be afraid of not knowing. God knows. That is all that matters.

Out of Nothing he creates Something. Out of the End he creates the Beginning. Out of selfness we grow, by his grace, toward selflessness, and out of that final selflessness, which is the loss of self altogether, "eye hath not seen nor ear heard, neither have entered into the heart of man" what new marvels he will bring to pass next. All's lost. All's found. And if such words sound childish, so be it. Out of each old self that dies some precious essence is preserved for the new self that is born; and within that child-self that is part of us all, there is perhaps nothing more precious than the fathomless capacity to trust.[3]

Perhaps the words of a wise and gentle child with a seemingly fathomless capacity to trust can shed some light for those of us who are older. Sarah Jean Kovar walked the entire length of her short life with hope. She died when she was eleven. But she never gave up.

Hi, boys and girls. My name is Sarah Jean Kovar and I have cancer. The reason I am writing this book to you is to share my experiences with you. So, if this ever happens to you, you will know what to expect.

Two things you need to get through all the things that happen in the course of cancer are faith and hope. Trust me, it will be hard going through life with cancer. But it will be tougher to get through without faith and hope. In fact, those are the two things I depend on most.

When I learned that a tumor had started to grow again, I thought I would never be able to get through life. But I knew that I had to have faith in the Lord. So as I did before, I handed my thoughts to the Lord.

I have to admit sometimes, I start to wonder if he's really helping me.

Then my mom reminds me of the things he has done for me. Then I realize that he really is helping me. So if you start to feel run-down, think of the Lord and of all the things he is doing and all he has done to help you.

Cancer is a killer. It is a very sad thing, but true. I plan to continue to fight for my life. Why don't you?[4]

Eleven-year-old Sarah wrote those words a few day before she died.

In life we will experience many Point Bs, small deaths, changes that involve personal loss or redefinition of self. We would be wise to heed the words of a "knowing" child. It is hard to experience loss, but it is tougher without faith and hope.

Someday I may learn that "a tumor has started to grow again." That is the reality of my life. I hope, if that day comes, I will show half the courage of little Sarah Jean Kovar. Her invitation to "fight for life—why don't you?" is a challenge to think of all the things the Lord is doing and has done to keep the faith; believe God's promises and trust him.

In the days to come, I intend to bend, shift, redefine, and become. In the words of little Sarah Jean Kovar, "Why don't you?"

Twelve

Transcendence

*"Some a'these days I'll be where i won't
have t'walk in th'mud"*

—Arie Carpenter
(92-year-old pioneer mountain woman),
Aunt Arie: A Foxfire Portrait

Love never fails.

—1 Corinthians 13:8

I could not believe it. Was this craziness or what? These days I am blaming most of my craziness on "The Change." But even I knew I could not chalk up this change to altering body chemistry. As the old saying goes, I did not even know when to come in out of the rain! There I was: sitting in the miserable cold, trying unsuccessfully to avoid blustery rain pellets under a flimsy umbrella, ignoring the distant lightning as if it did not really matter at all, screaming at the top of my lungs until my voice failed, high-fiving like a seasoned jock while I pounded my feet into the bleachers for maximum noise assault. And when I realized I was feeling as if eternity would be impacted in the next few minutes, it hit me: I had definitely gone over the edge. Oh yes, to my considerable amazement, I had become one of *them*: I was a football parent.

Horrors!

My hesitation to become a football parent has been rational—football is dangerous. For years our son had begged us to let him play. For years we refused, but he wore us down with his passionate persistence. Actually, we thought we were being crafty. We comforted ourselves that in the end, our permission to play would be a moot point: at 5'7" he would probably never get in a game! Why be a parental bad guy if you do not have to be?

I close my eyes a lot these days. I close my eyes when I watch him play. Apparently, one does not need to be big to play football. Although our son is the shortest kid on our team, it turns out he is also the fastest, which means, to my consternation, he carries the ball a lot. He assures me that this is an honor. He has not convinced me. What I am convinced of is the probability he will be injured. From a mother's perspective in the stands, all I see is the entire other team, converging like human homing missiles toward him. They snarl like starving flesh-eaters; sweat soaks through their equipment and down their muddy legs. My adrenaline signals "Flight!" I do not see teenage bodies; I see Mack trucks. Their go-for-the-kill attitudes make Mafia hit men seem like cultured gentlemen. They race after my son, diving and exploding into him, tackling him, and when they have him, they either throw him for yards like a rag or crunch his single body (which I so carefully birthed and cared for all these years) underneath their entire team.

Just because you are sitting in the bleachers does not mean you have the stuff to be a real football parent. Real football parents pray their sons will have the honor of playing. They complain if their sons are standing on the sidelines. My attitude was deplorable. When they put my son in I shouted, "Oh no! He's in!" "They" would look at me with shock on their faces, as if I had just yelled an obscenity or had publicly confessed to being a mass murderer. "They" knew I was not a "real" football parent.

A Night I Became a Real Football Parent

But this particular, amazing, rain-soaked night would even turn me into a crazy football parent. Our guys were playing a team that was ranked first in the state, ninth in the nation. We were a much smaller school, a much smaller team; we were supposed to lose, big time. The papers had announced the game as a "yawner."

It was the other school's homecoming, and they had invited us, assured that we would not spoil the festivities of their weekend. Much to everyone's amazement, we took an early lead and held them. Throughout what looked to be an incredible upset, their stands sat stunned and quiet, a picture of disbelief. Our stands, on the other hand, could not stay in their seats. Our boys were pumped. From the sidelines, they became their own cheerleaders, turning to us in the stands and punching their hands in the air indicating . . . MORE NOISE! Right! As if that were possible! They jumped all over each other and danced on the sidelines. They played with incredible heart and courage that night. They were winning . . . right up until the very last seconds. If there had been any poetic justice at all in this world, the other team would not have squeaked out a win in the end.

Our coaches cried afterward. Our boys had nothing left to cry with or they might have too. The professional TV announcers were way over the top, screaming and shouting into their microphones things like, "What a near upset! What heart these kids showed tonight! What a heartbreaker! Unbelievable!" They said the other team would definitely remember we had been there. They said they personally would never forget that game.

Who Are the Real Winners?

I suppose it was inevitable that we lost. It is a funny thing, though, this winning and losing business. I suspect that when people talk about that game in the future, they will not be talking about the win. They will not even talk much about the winning team. What they will talk about is us—the terrific fight our smaller underdog team gave the big team. They will talk about how tough we played. They will remember us as the team with the enormous heart. You see, the other team only walked away with the win, but we walked away with the glory.

It is like the Olympic credo states, "The essence lies not in the victory, but in the struggle." That is as true in life as it is in sports. It is often difficult to say who the real winners are. Sometimes real winners do not walk away with the ribbons or the medals or the trophies or the national rankings. Sometimes real winners lose, big time.

The Big-Time Loss

We do not like to think about it, but in time, we must all lose, big time. Inevitably, the days to come will include a life-and-death struggle. Regardless of the heart we show, in spite of the battle we put up, inevitably we will lose everything to death. Death will prove to be just too big, too strong, too mean.

C. S. Lewis wrote this personification of death, "Do not think you can escape me; do not think you can call me Nothing. To you I am not Nothing; I am the being blindfolded, the losing all power of self-defense, the surrender, not because any terms are offered, but because resistance is gone: the step into the dark: the defeat of all precautions: utter helplessness turned out to utter risk: the final loss of liberty."[1]

It is fashionable to be casual about death. It is modern to shrug and act as if death is "nothing" in the sense that it is normal, so we might as well accept it.

I, however, will never view death casually. Nor am I blasé about death's relative, disease. Both are evidences of an evil plan that seems to have all the genius of hell behind it. We were not created for death any more than we were born for senility or cancer or disease of any other kind. Death and disease are foreign concepts introduced by sin into our world, a world originally created for the continuance and sustenance of life. I will never accept them as natural or as a part of the life cycle or inevitable because "you are old, don't you know?" Death, particularly, is the final indignity. The last strike.

Furthermore, death is a personal assault. Just as life is the result of the creative genius of God, and our lives and the world we live in is no more haphazard than the lesser creations of man like a watch or a computer or a beautiful painting; so too our dying is not haphazard but the result of a personal assault of a creative, evil genius.

Additionally, our death is more than a personal struggle; it is also an unholy assault aimed at the very heart of God. Satan is not blasé about our dying. It is his great delight. The death of our bodies is his most hopeful joy, an indicator that he might, for the time being, be winning his ultimate battle—his battle against God. In death, Satan's pièce de résistance, as it were, he realizes his plan for our destruction, but he also hopes to strike a deeper blow; he hopes to strike at the heart of God.

Instead of a Loss, Death Becomes a Win

As consuming and powerful as death is, it is highly over-rated. Death has the win on the scoreboard. It has, in fact, reputedly never lost a game, but it can also never have the final word. For the soul, there is the possibility of transcendence. The person whose soul is rooted in God (the woman who understands that death's powerful hold has been broken for eternity by Jesus Christ's death, burial, and resurrection from the dead) can view even that most sad day to come—that day of the laying down of every facet of earthly life, that day of final surrender—as potentially a day of both tears and laughter. We will have the last laugh because death is the big-time loss through which we actually win.

C. S. Lewis spoke of the mixed bag called dying as,

On the one hand Death is the triumph of Satan, the punishment of the Fall, and the last enemy. Christ shed tears at the grave of Lazarus and sweated blood in Gethsemane: The Life of Lives that was in Him detested this penal obscenity not less than we do, but more. On the other hand, only he who loses his life will save it. We are baptized into the death of Christ, and it is the remedy for the Fall. Death is, in fact, what some modern people call "ambivalent." It is Satan's great weapon and also God's great weapon: it is holy and unholy; our supreme disgrace and our only hope; the thing Christ came to conquer and the means by which He conquered.[2]

In other words, in death as in life, it is difficult to tell who the real winners are. Sometimes the real winners lose big time. Death wins, but God's love will not fail us. Love never fails.

God's love transcends the power of death. Eternity will have the final interpretation, the last word about death.

Today Matters for Eternity

In light of this great eternal struggle, the battle between good and evil, God and Satan, life and death, how we live now matters for eternity. We participate daily in this struggle between our Enemy and God. We either encourage the Enemy and promote evil or struggle to live so that evil does not gain a foothold through our lives. A woman who refuses to live focused on her exterior self. A woman who has potential to be dangerously impacting on a spiritual level. A loving life, marked by acts of patient kindness, is more than the building of godly character; it strikes a blow at the enemy. It declares through consistent, loving deeds the loyalty of the lover toward God. An envious woman is not only eating out her own heart, but she is also advancing evil through her own attitudes and choices. Discipline the tendency to vaunt self and behave unseemly, and we have tamed more than self. We have tamed our evil potential. Our living, like our dying, is impacting on two levels: it is both personally spiritual and cosmically spiritual.

A Soul Goal: To Live as a Spiritually Dangerous Woman

The soul is capable of both great holiness and nearly complete corruption. Even when a woman loves God, she is still capable of playing for the evil side. The tended feminine soul is careful not to contribute to an evil agenda on any level, no matter how small. The soul can claim daily moral victory, even before heaven's final word. It is possible to live in such a way as to take the fun out of any win evil may eventually have.

There is nothing neutral about life. That is an attitude the Enemy promotes—spiritual naiveté. I know I have an Enemy. I intend to treat him as such. I do not want to live in defeat and in sin, giving my Enemy pleasure because he has used me to break God's heart. I definitely want to leave my mark, to get in my lick. I want to live in such a way that when I do die, evil will have known I had been here.

For the woman who believes that how she lives matters for eternity, for the woman who wants to leave a lasting impression, the urge to get into the game is strong. Even at the risk of being injured, she is willing to play for the sake of a greater cause. It is an honor to carry the spiritual ball. It is an honor to be converged on by the other side. It means you are carrying your weight. It means you are spiritually dangerous even if you are a small woman, with little obvious impact and considered non-threatening by those making projections.

We can join that remarkable laughing Proverbs 31 woman if we live with the understanding that many of our days to come will be experienced in heaven. Our life on earth may look like the final word, but it is only a chapter, not the entire book. "Some a'these days, you and I'll be where we won't have t'walk in th'mud," you know? The awareness that our intrinsic selves will not end at death can make all the difference in how we weather the present.

A View of Heaven Gives Perspective Today

What will heaven be like? If you talk to people about it, you can hear as many interpretations of heaven as people you ask. It seems that everyone has his or her own expectations of what it is going to be like.

We had guests over one night. It had been an evening of laughter. Our talk turned lightly to what heaven might be like. My extroverted husband, Steve, said that heaven would be like a giant beach party and all of his friends would be there. My oldest son, who can rarely get his family to invest hours and days into the kind of strategic games he likes to play, said, not surprisingly, that heaven was going to be an enormous strategy game and *everyone* would have to play. When it was my turn I said I pictured heaven to be like living on an African safari, except all the animals would be tame and you would not have to feed or clean up after them. They laughed at me and called me "Sheena of Heaven." I told you it was light!

As we went around the table, we enjoyed each other's interpretations of heaven that exposed who we were and the things that gave us joy. When we came to our guests' small son, he looked up with an innocent expression, his face covered with a chocolate-cake smile, and said, "I think heaven is going to be . . . *whenever* you want . . . you can get up in Jesus' lap!"

Leave it to a child to be theologically correct and spiritual too!

To anticipate heaven in terms of our own earthly joys should not be taken lightly. Whatever our personal grid, we know that heaven will be joy. Evil will have no foothold. We will be healed of all earthly pains. It will be a righteous kingdom where God will rule. Our souls will finally realize that all our earthly yearnings and longings were "prelongings" for the great longing of eternal intimacy with our God, our Soul Mate, the great lover of our souls. In heaven, our longings will be revealed as the Great Longing, and we will be satisfied.

Heaven is not just for eternity; it is for today as well. An eye on heaven can enormously impact the way we live on earth.

A mother told me this story about her son. He had become paralyzed in a car accident. He was only twenty-one at the time. All that remained of his movement was above his shoulders. He was devastated. He did not want to live in his condition. He cried constantly and asked to die. He became angry and sullen, withdrawing from all human contact. Mostly, though, he was angry with God.

His mother shared that she did not tell many people the next part of her son's story. "Too many cynics!" she sighed. This is what she told me. One night when her son could not sleep, a bright light appeared in his room from nowhere. Before he could scream or yell, he found himself ascending up . . . up . . . up . . .

In no time, he was in a place of incredible light. He saw his grandfather, who had recently died. He saw Jesus. He realized this place must be heaven. He ran to them, and then he realized: he was without his wheelchair. His head was held upright. His body had complete movement. He was strong. He ran and laughed, ran and cried.

Then, as suddenly as it had occurred, it was over. He was back in his room in his bed, back to being paralytic. He screamed for his mother and told her he had seen heaven and what he had experienced there. His mother thought initially he must have been dreaming, except that from then on, her son was a changed person. He wanted to live. His anger subsided. He laughed. He let others love him. He became interested in spiritual things. He understood that God loved him. He was able to love God back.

She asked me if I believed he could actually have had an out-of-the-body but still-in-the-body experience that had allowed him to experience heaven. (She believed it was possible.) I thought for a moment and said, "I really do not know what to make of it." With God anything is possible, after all. We agreed completely on one thing, however, and that was this: knowing that in heaven his body would be restored, having had even a small glimpse of the future possibilities of healing and strength, the up-close love of God had strengthened this young man enough to bear his earthly cross in his own body day after day. The question is not, did it *actually* happen? But did it *actually* make all the difference in his life?

The answer is yes! Even a small glimpse of heaven can help us bear the burdens of the present. Having one eye on eternity is the secret to being able to laugh at the days to come. Even in the face of certain death—the great evil that in time comes against us all—even then, a woman who keeps heaven in her perspective can laugh.

Fit Our Souls for Heaven Today

Today is more than the present. It is the time to fit our souls for heaven, to learn to love, to learn to be more than a polished cup, to close the gaps in our souls with spiritual integrity, to deepen and strengthen. It is time to get in a few licks against the other side before time runs out on the scoreboard. It is time to live with a soul awareness that connects to God's love and to others. It is also time to laugh.

I hear a tune. Our Enemy hears dancing music. He dances wildly to it, his feet trampling over our deathbeds and onto our graves with the bacchanalian joy of his win. He gloats, he revels, but his victory celebration is premature. He should pay closer attention. The joyful music is deceiving. The lyrics tell another story:

> *Be thou my Vision, O Lord of my heart;*
> *Naught be all else to me save that thou art—*

Thou my best thought by day or by night,
Waking or sleeping, thy presence my light.
Riches I need not, nor man's empty praise,
Thou my inheritance, now and always;
Thou and Thou only, first in my heart,
High King of heaven, my Treasure thou art.
High King of heaven, my victory won,
May I reach heaven's joys, O bright heav'n's Sun!
Heart of my own heart, whatever befall,
Still be my Vision, O Ruler of all.

The hymn, translated from Gaelic by Mary Byrne and versified by Eleanor Hull, is sung by the soul of a spiritual woman. It is a love song, not a funeral dirge. The singing is possible, even in death, because the woman has one eye on eternity. The Enemy was right to hear a win in the music but wrong to assume the victory was his.

Picture her. Her breath comes in gasps and rattles. Her eyes are glazed. Her neck can no longer support her head which leans to the side. Her hair is gone; her strength sapped. She is in her final struggle. No physical beauty remains. She can no longer fight. It is time to surrender. She too hears the music, senses the gleeful dancing of evil feet. Her dying is bringing them joy. She regrets that, but she has no power. Death will claim the win soon.

But even as she is losing one world, she is gaining another. The eyes of her soul seek heaven. As her memories pass in review, she recounts a lifetime of God's faithfulness, of love that never failed her. She has lived well. God has been so good. Confidence about her future floods over her. Fear subsides. It is time to make sure they will remember she came.

Then she does that crazy thing. She laughs. It is weak, but bold. She laughs right in the face of death. It is a holy sound that sends a shudder through the evil side. It confuses the revelers. Dancing stops; they are stunned and silenced. The soft but confident laughter drowns out their victory celebration.

Their win has become exceedingly hollow. They know she knows the truth. She knows what they know. Death is not the final word. The holy old woman, in her dying breath, has just accomplished an incredible coup de grace. She has had the last holy laugh. She has robbed them of their joy, taken the fun out of her suffering. Even in death love did not fail her.

In the eternal years to come, when they talk about her—and they will talk about her—they will not talk about her loss, but the great heart she brought to this struggle of living. Her beautiful soul, the love she brought to her living, the essence of her struggle—how she "gave it" to the evil side—will be the talk, the joyful laughing talk of eternity.

In heaven, you will have no trouble finding her. She will be the one sitting in Jesus' lap, laughing and laughing and laughing. The book ends, but it is not over, for she goes on. For all of eternity this sister to all of our feminine souls will have the last laugh.

Notes

Chapter 1: How Did Mother Get into My Mirror?

1. Maurice Jastrow, as quoted in Simone de Beauvoir's, *The Coming of Age* (New York: G. P. Putnam's Sons, 1972), 95.

2. Phillip L. Berman, *The Courage to Grow Old* (New York: Ballantine, 1989), 7.

3. Paul Theroux, "Self-Propelled," *US Air Magazine* (April 1994), 37.

Chapter 2: Soul Mirrors: Having Your True Colors Done by Trevor the Terrible

1. Sarah L. Delany and A. Elizabeth Delany with Amy Hill Hearth, *Having Our Say: The Delany Sisters' First 100 Years* (New York: Dell Publishing, 1993), 257.

2. William S. Stafford, *Disordered Loves: Healing the Seven Deadly Sins* (Boston: Cowley Publications, 1994), 82.

3. "Mrs. Congeniality May Have a Rather Nasty Background," *Chicago Tribune* 8 June 1995, Section 1, 25.

4. Thomas Moore, *Care of the Soul: A Guide for Cultivating Depth and Sacredness in Everyday Life* (New York: HarperCollins, 1992), 140.

5. William S. Stafford, *Disordered Lives*, 82–83.

Chapter 3: Soul Goals

1. H. Jackson Brown Jr., *Life's Little Instruction Book: 511 Suggestions, Observations, and Reminders on How to Live a Happy and Rewarding Life* (Nashville: Rutledge Hill Press, 1991), 435.

Chapter 4: Faux Soul

1. Thomas Moore, *Care of the Soul: A Guide for Cultivating Depth and Sacredness in Everyday Life* (New York: HarperCollins, 1992), Introduction, xvii-xviii.

2. Gregory of Nyssa, "The Life of Moses," in *The Classics of Western Spirituality*, trans. Abraham J. Malherbe and Everett Ferguson (New York: Paulist,

1987), 137. As quoted in Richard J. Foster, *Prayer: Finding the Heart's True Home* (San Francisco: HarperCollins, 1992), 150.

3. Richard J. Foster, *Prayer: Finding the Heart's True Home* (San Francisco: HarperCollins, 1992), 195.

4. Dick Eastman, "How To Spend An Hour In Prayer," *Leadership* (Winter 1982), 90.

5. George Appleton, *The Oxford Book of Prayer* (Oxford, NY: Oxford University Press, 1985), 158.

6. Ibid., 160.

Chapter 5: Color Me Patient, Color Me Kind

1. Dan B. Allender, *The Wounded Heart: Hope for Adult Victims of Childhood Sexual Abuse* (Colorado Springs: NavPress, 1990), 198.

2. Robertson McQuilkin, "Muriel's Blessing," *Christianity Today* (February 5, 1996), 32–34. Used by permission.

3. L. Morris, *I Corinthians* in *Tyndale New Testament Commentaries* (Downers Grove, Ill.: InterVarsity Press, 1958), 181. As quoted in David Prior, *The Message of I Corinthians* (Downers Grove, Ill.: InterVarsity Press, 1985), 226.

4. C. S. Lewis, *Mere Christianity*, as quoted in Wayne Martindale and Jerry Root, *The Quotable Lewis* (Wheaton, Ill.: Tyndale House, 1989), 402.

5. Gloria Hutchinson, *Six Ways To Pray From Six Great Saints* (Cincinnati: St. Anthony Messenger Press, 1982), 87. As quoted in Richard J. Foster, *Prayer: Finding the Heart's True Home* (San Francisco: HarperCollins, 1992), 62–63.

6. Ibid.

7. Frederick Buechner, *Listening to Your Life: Daily Meditations With Frederick Buechner* (San Francisco: HarperCollins, 1992), 302. © 1992 by Frederick Buechner. Used by permission.

Chapter 6: It's Not Easy Being Green

1. Regina Barreca, "Envy," *Chicago Tribune Magazine* 19 March 1995, Section 10, 28.

2. As quoted in "To Illustrate," *Leadership* (Fall 1990), 48.

3. Wilfred Sheet, *In Love With Daylight* (Simon and Schuster) as quoted in *The Reader's Digest* (August 1995), 37.

4. "Give Thanks" © 1978 Integrity's Hosanna Music. Used by permission.

Chapter 7: Red-Hot Mamas I've Known and Been

1. Charles Derber, *The Pursuit of Attention: Power and Individualism in Everyday Life* (New York: Oxford Press, 1979), 22, 23.
2. William S. Stafford, *Disordered Lives: Healing the Seven Deadly Sins* (Boston: Cowley Publications, 1994), 120.
3. Melita Marie Garza, "Last Heat Victims Buried with No One to Mourn Them," *Chicago Tribune* 26 August 1995, Section 1, 1.

Chapter 8: Club Snob

1. Elliot Wigginton and Margie Bennett, *Foxfire 9* (New York: Doubleday, 1985), 438–51.

Chapter 9: A Tree Grows in Wheaton

1. Lewis B. Smedes, *Forgive and Forget: Healing the Hurts We Don't Deserve* (San Francisco: HarperCollins, 1984), Introduction.
2. Ibid., 132–133.
3. Helen Roseveare, *He Gave Us a Valley* (Downers Grove, Ill: InterVarsity Press, 1976), 35–36.

Chapter 10: "Younging"

1. Reuters, "At 120 Years Plus 238 Days, It's a Record," *Chicago Tribune* 16 October 1995, Section 1, 8.

Chapter 11: Changes and Becomings

1. Sheila Walsh, *Honestly* (Grand Rapids: Zondervan, 1996), 22–33.
2. Gregory of Nyssa, "The Life of Moses," in *The Classics of Western Spirituality*, trans. Abraham J. Malherbe and Everett Ferguson (New York: Paulist, 1987), 137. As quoted in Richard J. Foster, *Prayer: Finding the Heart's True Home* (San Francisco: HarperCollins, 1992), 150.
3. Frederick Buechner, *Listening to Your Life* (San Francisco: HarperCollins, 1992), 174. © 1992 by Frederick Buechner. Used by permission.
4. Sarah Jean Kovar, *My Journey of Hope: A Child's Guidebook for Living with Cancer* (Grand Rapids: Zondervan, 1993).

Chapter 12: Transcendence

1. C. S. Lewis, *The Pilgrim's Regress*, as quoted in Wayne Martinsdale and Jerry Root, *The Quotable Lewis* (Wheaton, Ill: Tyndale House, 1989), 143.
2. Ibid., 145–46.

Re: Valerie Bell's Public Appearances

If you are interested in inquiring about Valerie Bell speaking for your church, organization, or special event, please contact:

>*Attn:* Valerie Bell
>P. O. Box 1399
>Wheaton, IL 60189
>Phone/Fax: 630/668-8412

Re: Valerie Bell's *Prayer*WALK
audio aerobic/prayer cassette tapes

To order copies of any of the *Prayer*WALK cassette tapes listed below, please specify your request(s) and send check payment to:

Valerie Bell • P.O. Box 1399 • Wheaton, IL 60189

Item No.	Title	Price
PW-031194	PrayerWalk . . . Care for Body and Soul	$11.95
PW-119601	PrayerWalk II . . . Praise: The Practice of Heaven	$11.95
PW-970101	Classic PrayerWalk . . . Blessing Your Community	$11.95

The cost of each cassette tape is noted above. Plus, add a $2.00 shipping/handling fee for one cassette tape copy. (For 2-5 copies the s/h fee total is $3.50; for 6-10 copies the s/h fee total is $5.00; for 11 or more copies the s/h fee total is $8.00.) Upon receipt of payment, your tape(s) will be mailed out as quickly as possible. Of course, be sure to include your complete address.

Walk with God!

DATE DUE
